For our guests

Paul Vermeul

Utrecht 2000

The construction of meaning in sport organizations:

Management of diversity

The construction of meaning in sport organizations:

Management of diversity

Annelies Knoppers (Ed.)

SHAKER PUBLISHING BV

Printed in The Netherlands

ISBN 90-423-0108-2

Photograph cover: J. de Boer

Cover design and lay-out: R. van Wijnen and J. Thoben

Shaker Publishing BV
St. Maartenslaan 26
6221 AX Maastricht
Tel: 043-3500424
Fax: 043-3255090
http://www.shaker.nl

Contents

Foreword

General membership meeting Synergus

The person chairing the first general membership meeting of the club Synergus is unknown to most of the approximately hundred members attending. He is a last minute replacement for the current chair who has just announced (in a letter) that he has quit. The minutes of the last meeting cannot be found. The members refuse to accept the final report describing the past year. A member explains: 'It contains very little about last year; instead it contains quite a few personal opinions of the new secretary about the new situation.'

After this tumultuous and disorganized beginning, the tension rises in the meeting. It is time to appoint new council members and the current council is incomplete. A group of eight people has declared their candidacy and want to form a totally new council. This alternate council includes the chair of the former Donaro club and her sponsor. This former Donaro chair has lost the power struggle with the former chair of Bunder about who has a say in the new club after the merger. The former Donaro chair sees the alternate council as an opportunity to regain some of his power since the council of the new club is incomplete and has received much criticism from the members. The current council, however, does not give up that easily. It does not want to step aside for a new council. A very emotional and heated discussion follows in which many old wounds are reopened. Those members of the top men's team who are present threaten not to play in Sunday's match. The decision is made to vote to decide which of the two councils will hold office. The chaos is complete after the ballots have been distributed, because it is unclear what the members are voting on. Someone behind the bar plays the music of André Hazes ('A little bit in love') at top volume. The chair of the meeting gives up.

Introduction: What is going on?

Sport clubs are under a great deal of pressure. Historically, sport clubs have been social- cultural bastions in which individuals voluntarily come together out of love for sport. Sport clubs are often places where individual, sport en societal developments take place. They are assumed to contribute to social integration and therefore, to societal cohesion. However, the developments

7

that contribute to the disintegration of society, also affect these clubs. Many sport clubs, some of whom have a tradition going back more than a hundred years, barely manage to survive. The meanings assigned to sport and membership in a sport club, have changed. 'Loose ties' seem to be replacing 'unconditional loyalty' and love for the sport club. Members are beginning to look and behave more like clients. Athletes sometimes fail to show up for their match. When they do show up, their relationship with the referee and the opponent often erupts in controversy. Professionals are replacing volunteers in the clubs. General membership meetings, which used to mirror the democratic nature of the club, are poorly attended and replaced by committees of 'experts.' Clubs manage to avoid losses by attracting sponsors and gifts from wealthy members.

In short, club ties are changing. According to scholars, societal trends towards individualism and rationalism are affecting the sport club as well. According to sport managers, members see themselves as consumers (Anthonissen & Boessenkool, 1998). According to the authors of this book, the processes involved in the construction or assignment of meanings play an important role in organizational life and need to be examined. In other words, the problems cited above need to be analyzed in the context of organizational and societal developments. This means we need to explore the processes of integration (consensus), differentiation (differences) and fragmentation (ambiguity), and most of all, the meanings that these processes have in the lives of individuals.

Sense making

Sport and sport clubs are assumed to play an important role in fostering belonging and integration. Belonging is an essential aspect of life yet it is based on making distinctions. Sport in other words, also creates difference. Athletes recognize each other as such but it makes a difference if you play football or play chess, if you are member of DESTO or RKWK, if you are a fan of Manchester United or Manchester City. Sport can foster loyalty and create boundaries whether a person actively participates or is a fan/supporter. Sport can integrate and differentiate. Who is excluded or included is related to processes of sense making in sport organizations and in the broader societal context.

Sport is part of society. It is affected by developments in other sectors of society such as home life, the labour market, education, and by processes such as globalization, inclusion/ exclusion and commercialization. Meanings assigned to sport, affect other parts of society as well. The meanings the media assign to male black physicality may for example, dominate the stereotypes we have about black males in general (Knoppers & Elling, 1999a). In other words, meanings are constructed in sport that subsequently may influence the way individuals construct meanings in other parts of society. Conversely, societal processes affect sport but in ways that may be unique to sport settings. The problems of old sport bastions and the simultaneous increase in interest in sport by societal actors such as government and businesses are part of the interactive process of sense making about and in sport. The manner in which integration (cohesion), difference (differentiation) and ambiguity (fragmentation) are given a place in sport organizations is dependent on the way in which meanings in society and in institutional sport, interact with individual meanings, that is, the extent to which they include or exclude each other, change each other, are combined to create new combinations of meanings, etc. Sense making in sport organizations is therefore, an interactive process between different actors and various social cultural aspects. In this book we look at the ways in which meanings are produced in sport and reproduced in the context of this complex interaction.

We begin this book by sketching perspectives on sense making (chapter 1) and on (sport) organizations and society (chapter 2). In the following chapter (chapter 3) we explore the extent to which perspectives on organizations and on sport are gendered and the influence this gendering has on sense making in sport organizations. In the following four chapters we examine processes of the construction of meaning in various sport situations using case studies (based on more extensive research studies). The case study approach may make each topic readily recognizable for the reader. We begin with a chapter (chapter 4) that explores the way in which the sport managers cope with the movement towards professionalization of sport clubs. They often use the argument that 'to do well at the top, we need a broad base' (pyramid), to convince members that a major share of the club's resources is to be used for the top men's team. We examine how sport managers attempt to ensure that this idea, a common one in sport, becomes the dominant discourse and we explore the ways in which that discourse is challenged. Other clubs use a merger to respond to the situation sketched in the beginning of this chapter. The fifth chapter describes the process of the merger of two clubs. Meanings assigned to sport and club membership within each club prior to the merger cannot be ignored but new meanings must also be constructed.   How do sport managers handle this and 'build' a new sport club?

Societal changes do more than nudge clubs towards professionalization and/ or mergers. Processes of internationalization or globalization of the economy and of immigration within a country, result in new intercultural connections. The incorporation of other nationalities and the differences among first, second and third generations of immigrants present challenges to sport clubs. How do processes of integration and differentiation develop and how are meanings about sameness and about difference constructed in different sport clubs? Chapter 6 explores meanings assigned to integration and ethnicity within the sport context. The impact of internationalism is not, however, confined to sport clubs within the Netherlands, but also pertains to relations Dutch sport organizations have with sport organizations in other countries. The relationship between projects in sport and international cooperative development shows how making sense of sport is dependent on the context. In chapter 7 we examine the construction of meanings in a sport project involving actors from the Netherlands and South Africa. To what extent can mutual understanding be developed and what meanings do the various relationships have for the actors themselves?

In the closing chapter (chapter 8) we explore the themes underlying these case studies: what do they tell us about the construction of meaning in sport organizations and in sport itself? We then look at possible perspectives that may help sport managers in understanding and working with the various processes of sense making in sport and sport organizations.

Paul Verweel

Sense making in sport organizations

Overview

In this chapter I give an overview of our theoretical approach to this study of sense making in sport organizations. We will first 'listen' to athletes interact with each other as they assign meanings about the match they just finished playing. An examination of the cultural meanings constructed by these athletes (and those in sport organizations) requires us to explore the processes involved in sense making. I argue that culture not only means agreement (integration) but also difference (differentiation) and even antagonism and ambiguity (fragmentation) among individuals. The question of integration, differentiation and fragmentation is a starting point for describing and understanding the dynamics within organizations themselves. I then look at the process of sense making itself and the levels (individual, structural and social) at which that process occurs.

The Third Half

This exchange took place in the restaurant of a football club after the fifth senior men's team of DESTO finished their match. After showering, the athletes take their places around a large square table. The initial fatigue of the match has been washed away with the first round of soft drinks and beer. They begin to reflect on and replay the match: the third half.

Paul: Hey Pete, for a moment I thought I saw Martin in action.

Pete: What do you mean???

Paul: The time when Martin saw a unique chance to score against CJVV while standing on the goal line. You however, were already over the line when you shot the ball out of the goal of the opponent. When it happened with Martin, he left the field but you perhaps were hoping for a repeat. By the way, too bad he doesn't play anymore.

Bas (laughing): Hey, Pete, did the opponents treat you to a beer already? See, they want you to come and sit with them.

Pete: Now that you mention it, I must admit that you placed that ball quite accurately on my leg. The goal is seven meters wide, man!! I should have known better because in practice last week you couldn't hit anything either.

John: Yes, just like Tony today. Boy oh boy, I have rarely seen anyone touch so few balls and when he did touch them, they went to the opponent. By the way, has anyone seen him?

Hank: No, he really regretted his play. Normally he can take criticism but when you said that we were playing orange football he got angry. He went home because he had to do some errands.

Paul: Shopping? Anyone who is any sort of [male] athlete doesn't go to town Saturday to shop with his wife and the rest of the world. Saturday is for football.

John: You are right. We may have lost with 5-1 but we haven't had time to vandalize bus shelters. Still, I am upset after losing so badly.

Pete: Well, that penalty shot of mine was a good one.

Hank: You mean you calculated that the ball would ricochet into the goal from the pole against the head of the goalie. You probably were wearing your shoes on the wrong feet.

Hank: Does anyone want anything more to drink?

Bert: Yes, and add a bowl of snacks because I am treating because it is my birthday.

Hank: Congratulations, but this round is on me. I will place the order.

Jake: Hey guys, I have to submit a list of who will play in this team next year. Everyone, right?

John: I want to play as long as we do not get any new players who can't touch a ball. If we lose a few of the current players then only ex-top players can join.

Bas: I am thinking about stopping. I have to go the USA for a few months for my work. We are opening a branch there.

Paul: Don't whine, Bas. You belong here. Do you want to spend the rest of your time doing errands in the city??? I have to go to the USA for a month also. You cannot desert the team.

Jake: Everyone another round of beer and Paul another coke?

John: OK, this is the last round; Jake, make sure Paul doesn't get drunk on his coke.

Pete: A few guys at work want to start their own team at another club. They asked me to join.

Paul: I'm sure they won't let you take the penalty shots there, Pete, so stay. You aren't going to desert us for another club, are you? How long have you been a member here? Would you really want to join a kickers' club??

Bas: Hey, will Tony continue to play? He often has to work in the weekends in his new job and his wife has been sick several times lately.

Paul: That is probably the reason why he played so badly today but normally we need him. Tony is a good guy. Too bad he never stays around after a game but still . . ..

Jake: Guys, another round.

John: This is really the last one, Jake.

Paul: Look, the opponents are leaving. Hey, look at that bloke walk! He kicks everyone and then cries when he gets pushed. The referee is quite gullible. He probably learned the rules through a correspondence course.

John: Yes Paul, you know you can go as far as the referee lets you. The referee determines the limits of how far you can go. If you gab a bit with the guy he won't call you on so many things. You however keep commenting on his calls; no wonder he whistled against you so often.

Paul: Listen John, that dummy has to know the rules. What that midfielder did . . . if someone from our team would do something like that . . . I would stop playing.

Bas: Me too. That guy is blind . . . it is terrible to have such a guy on the field. According to me, even his teammates are ashamed of him.

Paul: But of course they didn't say anything and just played on.

Hank: Listen to yourself. Five years ago we were champions because you fell down in the penalty area. I thought you would never stand up again.

John: The opponents were so angry that that almost happened.

Paul: Wow, those guys of the opposing team were really upset . . . but it was more fatigue than anything else, I think. I think I am going home.

John: Come on, Paul, one more round and then we'll go. I will treat one more time so we can forget this embarrassing loss. Hey Pete, will you practice taking penalty shots some more?

After two more rounds they leave and go home because Uncle Case, the bar tender closes the bar.

An analysis of the Third Half: Making sense of a football match

Although the Third Half occupies only a page in this book, it would probably fill several volumes over the course of a season. The Third Half means a lot to its participants and fulfills several functions/ purposes simultaneously. It strengthens the relationships among the athletes and extends to other areas of life which mean much to the athletes.

The Third Half contains several stories varying in content and often having different functions.

 1) There is the story about Martin's loss. Pete's action enables them to recall a memory that includes him again.

2) Pete's action brings disappointment but gives a new story for the future.

3) The talk about shopping and the destruction of bus stops introduces the broader societal context.

4) Pete's penalty shows that Pete can enjoy himself while everyone is disappointed in the loss. Hank's remark makes the penalty acceptable but Pete is not allowed to openly enjoy his penalty when the team has lost.

5) Drinking and eating together is an important group happening which strengthens the sense of group identity. Paul's coke suggests, and at the same time challenges, that beer drinking is the norm. Paul is allowed to drink coke because he is part of the team but the implicit norm is that a football player is a beer drinker.

6) In the discussion about continuing the team, the mechanisms of exclusion become visible. Although current members are getting on in age, only new 'good' players are welcome. The ties among the members (inclusion) are also confirmed because those who do not want to continue are threatened with having to go shopping instead.

7) The discussion about the 'rules' shows how the rules are continually being reconstructed during the game and afterwards. Not the 'rules' but the interactions with the referee and with the opponent are decisive. The football players delineate (un) acceptable boundaries for behavior on the field by pointing to the behavior of the opposing midfielder.

The discussion in the Third Half does not have a general theme. Some meanings are reproduced and new meanings are constructed. Game situations stimulate production and reproduction of meanings that extend beyond the actual game. Team feeling and the roles the different players play, are continually 'negotiated' with use of the different topics and the ritual of buying another round. Being together enables the athletes to absorb the loss of the match (or enjoy the victory). Before leaving the sport world, the athletes share the various experiences in the match with those who understand without needing agreement from each other. The implicit 'rules' about who belongs and who does not and about which behaviors are acceptable, are reinforced. The nonsport experiences (shopping, destruction of bus stops and paid work) are woven into talk about the way the men experience sport, the team and the club. These hidden functions are probably more important for the individual experience and sense making than the actual content of the discussion.

The men come from a variety of backgrounds (from church goer to atheist, from liberal to communist, from car mechanic to professor, from bachelor to father with four children). This means that various fields of meaning are brought to the match. During the match the sport skills of the players dominate. During the Third Half recollections of those skills and their contribution to individual and social meanings dominate their interactions. Various communication styles are used to accomplish this sense making. The discussion has primarily a teasing tone but shifts between joking and seriousness. At times a joke or humor is used to get the message across. In the rest of this chapter and also in chapter 3, the Third Half is used as an illustration of the way interactions (re) produce meanings and create culture.

The sense making approach to organizations: Construction of meaning

Organizations, including those in the sport, are the result of complex interactions among individuals. Every day the organization is produced and reproduced not only in a material but also in a mental way. The importance of the construction of meaning in looking at organizations has its roots in the cultural approach. Ouchi (1978) and Peters & Waterman (1982) have provided the impetus for looking at the cultural aspects of organizations. Nonmaterial and technical aspects of the organizations came to be seen as critically important to the functioning of the organization. Du Gay (1977) even classifies economic activities of the organization as 'cultural.' (p. 137). I define culture as including cohesion (including prescriptions for action), the ideology of groups (Trice & Beyer, 1993; Douglas, 1982), the intensity of within- group relations (including the degree of prescribed behavior), the institutionalization of prescribed behavior into structures, and, the process by which some meanings become dominant and others are marginalized.

The cultural approach traces the relationship between the ideas/ideology people have and the ways in which they give them form and content (Trice & Beyer, 1993). This includes dominant and marginalized ideas, formal and informal regulations, interactions, and, the solidification of ideas in structures. The cultural approach assumes that the social cohesion of groups is associated with a certain degree of shared meanings, actions and structures. Individuals use these to organize their material and mental worlds. This arrangement is not just a question of categorization but also includes moral values. The method of arranging makes clear what is good and bad, who belongs and who does not, and, what is desirable and what is not.

The cultural approach is very popular among managers of organizations due to the belief that 'strong' culture will increase the loyalty of organizational members to the organization. Increased loyalty is assumed to enhance results. This assumption has led, for example, to the idea of creating 'corporate culture' for an organization. In the creation of 'corporate culture', efforts are made to have meanings constructed 'in community'. This implies that eventually, everyone will have the same perspective. This is assumed to enhance group cohesion, exemplified by shared values and norms.

Scholars have critiqued the corporate culture approach. Martin (1992) and Koot and Hogema (1992) argue that social cohesion does not just rest on shared meanings but also on disagreement among people and groups, and, on ambiguities in relationships. Integration (consensus), differentiation (differences) and fragmentation (ambiguity) each produce social cohesion but in different ways. In the following paragraphs I will explain each of these three models in detail.

Three perspectives for sense making in organizations

Each of the three models points to other processes of inclusion and exclusion. They appear in all organizations. Individuals may react to each other and assign meanings using the different models. In this sense, the organization is an arena of possible meanings.

Integration model

The integration model assumes the necessity of having a central organizational goal, a hierarchical structure, team work, and consensus. People accept a centralized authority and hierarchy. They work together to come to a consensus about the what, who, how and why of their organization. The resulting interactions and the meanings assigned to them are based on this consensus and stimulate the cohesion of the organization. The degree to which meanings are shared (plus the production of goods and services) becomes a defining factor for success. The integration perspective assumes that the organization as a whole has a strong boundary, has no internal divisions and 'forces' its ideas on others. The ideal 'corporate culture' is a variation of this theme.

Differentiation model

The differentiation model describes reality in a different way. This model assumes a struggle for power, competition among members of an organization, conflicts, self interest and dissent. Competition and conflict are seen as a result of different (self) interests. The course and direction of the organization are based on short or long term coalitions between different parties. Cohesion evolves out of the antagonism between individuals and groups who in a sense, rise to the occasion. The direction and course of the organization are determined by agreement on necessary qualities and interests that have survived the competition. The organization consists of many subcultures that grow out of differences or agreements in the construction of meanings and interests of the actors. The agreements are based on meanings that may be exclusive or inclusive compared to those of other individuals and groups. The differentiation approach assumes that there is no strong boundary between the organization and the 'outside', that it has strong internal boundaries that vary per group but also that each group has its shared way of interpreting reality. The organization is divided but the groups are not.

Fragmentation

Martin (1992) argues that there is room for a third model, fragmentation. She points out that in the differentiation model actors organize themselves (in small groups) that are themselves based on hierarchy, consensus and team work. The differentiation model describes actors at the organizational level but not at the individual or group level. In this post modern time, when ties within groups are becoming weaker (allowing the individual more freedom of action), the processes of fragmentation/ individualization need to be taken seriously. The fragmentation model pays attention to the increasing ambiguity in concepts and relationships in group and organizational processes. Cohesion is less dependent on institutional and group meanings and more on individual and intersubjective meanings. In any case, the individual has more freedom to reflect on (and separate themselves from) the dominant definitions of the institutions. The fragmentation perspective assumes that the outside boundaries of the organization and of the different groups are weak but offers the possibility of connecting people by way of a strong perspective that exceeds boundaries.

Sharing experiences and meanings

I assume that interactions are influenced by the use of the different models that in turn influence each other. Every culture is marked by a degree of group interaction and a degree of agreement in the meanings used. According to Frost & Smirchich (1983), Martin (1992) and Koot and Hogema (1992), making integration and shared meaning synonymous with cohesion fails to recognize the complexity of cultural relations and group/organizational ties. Attachment develops in the acceptance of meanings, in the tension between several meanings, and, in the space allotted for fuzzy concepts that arise due to differences in perceptions.

The assumption that cohesion means agreement on meanings can ironically be counterproductive for cohesion. DuGay (1995) sees this assumption as an ideological project in which the perspective of the management is confirmed as the dominant and desirable perspective. Meanings of others are welcome as long as they reinforce the perspective of management. We see examples of this in the various case studies. In this book we assume that cohesion contains elements of integration, differentiation and fragmentation that are more like forces that work beside and through each other in an organization and in society, than that they are categories that can be used to describe organizations.

The 'feeling of belonging' is not necessarily only found in the agreement about sense making but in the sharing of experiences. The sharing of experiences, despite the degree to which there is agreement about the meanings assigned to them, creates the 'ties' that binds people to each other. Being there when it happens is more important than a shared view on what happens. As Weick (1995) states: 'Although people may not share meaning, they do share experience' (p.188). He argues that differences in personal histories make the construction of shared meanings almost impossible. The repetition of (daily) experiences more often (re)produces social ties than the explicit sharing of (implicit) meanings.

Although the way individuals make sense of shared experiences may create significant differences among them, the sharing of experiences works as a powerful force to enhance social ties. Differences in meanings in the nonsport world, for example, may be easier to accept due to the shared experiences in sport and vice versa. The shared experience enables individuals to articulate and understand differences in the construction of meaning. Each individual meaning receives a place in the shared meanings. [1] Clearly each recall of the experience ties a group together although the members differ in their opinions about it. This means that in each conversation, like the Third Half, there is a search for a shared formulation that allows individual meanings to be articulated or be visible. The situation and the history of the group determine the extent to which this formulation is unambiguous, contradictory or fuzzy.

A description of organizational culture requires the creation of a new coherent structure of meanings out of a set of incoherent and disorderly events. This occurs in conversations with others because culture is essentially social and interactive. The concept 'organization' is not so much explained in the often used characteristics such as structure, formal goals, rules, prescribed behavior and production, but in the meanings that individuals assign to aspects of their social and material (re)production. The organization itself is a construction of meanings. Organizational cultures are recognizable in the stories of members of the organization. These stories are usually based on three important themes: 1) how things should go, 2) what is important, and, 3) who the heroes are (see also Du Gay, 1995, p. 153). The stories also express the 'natural' order, the facts of life and/or how life is organized here. Tennekes (1999) explains that these stories define the symbolic order in why, how and what and describe those who belong and those who do not. Stories, such as the Third Half, define the actors and their qualities.

Those who wish to change organizations have to influence the organizational and individual stories, rearrange those stories, add new ones (concepts and metaphors) and, in interaction with other members, create new structures for making sense of many incoherent and chaotic events in the present and in the past. Having new experiences and assigning meaning to them is therefore unavoidable. Organizational members continually try to make sense of their experiences. In this book we lean heavily on the concept of construction of meaning and sense making. How does this process of making sense work?

Frames

Verweel & David (1995), point to the creation and existence of cultural regimes in organizations and societies. Cultural (and political) regimes form a framework for interpretation that continually mediates our relation with reality. This framework includes perceptions of the world outside the organization, of client satisfaction, and, of the qualities of our own organization and of ourselves. A frame gives meaning to perceptions and determines actions. Perceptions and the associated actions are therefore mediated by our own frames of meaning. This implies that organizational processes and the organization itself are imagined. They exist only because we believe they exist or insist they exist.

In essence, reality consists of a variety of frameworks used for sense making. The construction of meanings is a continuous process that can only be understood in the context of social ties and the broader social context in which they are produced. The Dutch, for example, have a refined system for categorizing 'rain', the Inuit for 'snow' and others for the color 'green.' Frames emerge out of a human need to try to bring order out the chaos of impressions (Weick, 1995). Individuals need a certain amount of structure to attain a minimal level of certainty and safety. They partially achieve this by building up routines (regimes) for actions and perceptions. These routines are based on meanings that individuals construct themselves or take over from others. 'Frames and cues can be thought of as vocabularies in which words that are more abstract (frames) include and point to other less abstract words (cues) that become sensible in the context created by the more inclusive words. Meaning within the vocabularies is relational. A cue in a frame is what makes sense not the cue alone or the frame alone' (Weick, 1995, p. 110).

The understanding of new experiences is 'prestructured' by the already existing meanings and the existing regimes (see also du Gay, 1997). Changes in culture therefore, often involve the adaptation of existing routines. Resistance against cultural change flows (logically) from the fear of possibly losing the safety, security and certainty about the 'why, how and who' in the organization or in society.

Levels of meanings

In the Third Half we see the four levels through which organizations and frames are structured.

- First, individuals construct meanings.

- Second, those meanings are transformed in group interactions, that is, in the social intersubjective meanings that individuals construct with each other while in groups.

- Third, meanings are also embedded and absorbed into the structure of the organization and of society. At this level, the stories are not about individuals but about the occupants of specific positions. People are assigned identities according to their roles and positions.

- At the fourth level meanings are no longer associated with a 'knowing subject' (Popper cited in Weick, 1995, p. 72) but have become an abstraction, such as, for example, a concept as 'organizational culture' or 'organizational goals.' Yet this abstraction is never totally separated from the social group who created it, as Knoppers (chapter 3 of this book) points out.

Organizational life and organizations can be defined by the results of the way actors connect (or, do not connect) these four levels with each other. An organization is a social cultural construction created by actors in which the four levels of assigning meanings cited above are 'absorbed.'

Weick (1995) argues that language, perceptions and agency are related in the process of sense making. He says: 'If people know what they think, when they see what they say, then words figure in every step. Words impose discrete labels on subject matters . . . They approximate the territory; they never map it perfectly (p.107). This means that the logic in words, decisions and activities is constructed after the fact. We reflect on what happened to determine the what, why and who. Meanings are born in (inter) actions; when they are expressed in words they attain a language dimension and can then be discussed.

Words impose labels on subject matters and form part of a discourse. A discourse is everything said, written and conveyed about a particular topic. Although there is a dominant discourse, there are always alternate discourses, most of which are usually marginalized. The dominant discourse reflects or creates a dominant ideology and is presented as common sense and obvious (hegemonic). Discourses are frames or systems of meanings and indistinguishable from social practices; in other words, discourses evolve from practices or actions and discourses give words and images that facilitate practices (Tolson, 1996). Actions or practices therefore, do not only follow words. Sense making is an active and continuous process in which words and actions or practices constitute (and reconstitute) each other. The changing of practices therefore requires changing the meaning of words. Creating new definitions requires (inter) actions.

Events, cues and frames play a role in interactions. Weick (1995) says 'Frames and cues can be thought of as vocabularies in which words that are more abstract (frames) include and point to other less abstract words (cues) that become sensible in the context created by the more inclusive words. Meaning within the vocabularies is relational. A cue in a frame is what makes sense, not the cue alone or the frame alone. Sense making starts with three elements: a frame, a cue and a connection' (p. 110). This does not mean that there are no links between the past and the present; on the contrary, they are connected. 'Frames tend to be moments of past socialization and cues tend to be present moment of experience. Meaning is created when individuals can construct a relation between these two moments. This means that the content of sense making is to be found in the frames and categories [regimes] that summarize past experience, in the cues and labels that snare specific present moments of experience, and in the way these two settings of experience are connected' (p.111).

This chapter gives a framework for looking at sense making and also a strategy for locating vehicles and sites involved in sense making processes. This means that when we look at organizations we not only have to listen to individual stories and the intersubjective aspects but also have to look at the levels of meaning assigned in the (sport) organization and society. Frames, cues and connection occur not only at the subjective and interaction level but assume a broader meaningful context in the process of sense making, in other words, they assume an actor in context as we will see in the following chapters.

Paul Verweel and Arie de Ruijter

Perspectives on organization and society

Overview

In this chapter we look at organizational and societal contexts of sense making of the sport experience. In the foreword to this book we described the dominant perceptions of sport managers that athletes have little loyalty for the club and that clubs face many problems. These observations pertain not only to sport but are embedded in a broader societal context. The call for (unified) cohesion is a dominant one in society. Politicians, just like sport managers, perceive a lack of connection between the individual citizen and groups. A feeling of crisis dominates. The cry for connection, for clarity in values and norms, and for socialization into those norms and values, is heard everywhere. What are the underlying developments and frames that can be used to make sense of these developments?

We assume that sport organizations are half-open systems, which means that they are influenced by the broader societal context. It also means that many societal processes receive a unique shape and content within sport. The interaction between sport organizations and society occurs along two lines. First, the interaction between persons is bound by legal and social rules. Second, there are the rules (such as those about membership dues and classification based on gender) that determine who may take part in sport and in the debates within a club and who are the significant others (stakeholders) for the club and sport managers. Members always bring their societal perspectives and rules with them to the club. The degree to which they apply societal rules depends on their interactions within the sport and the club.

We review the question of social cohesion in society along the perspectives of integration, differentiation and fragmentation as they have been put forth in the debate over globalization and localization of society (Wallerstein, 1975; Hannertz, 1992). In this scholarly debate the answer is sought in the tension and connection between the processes of international equality and the need for profiling the 'self.' Connection and uniqueness are seen as two sides of the same medallion.

In the tension among the characteristics of integration and differentiation we find a framework for describing several empirical processes in sport organizations. Both perspectives give insights into the ways in which socialization tendencies and the need for the development of own identity and practices of individuals and groups can be understood. Stated in the terms of our cultural meaning approach: in the dynamic of integration and differentiation thinking, a new frame/regime evolves that, together with new cues, leads to new sense making processes in sport and in sport organizations.

Society: Consensus making or coordination

As we suggested earlier, politicians and some social scientists perceive a lack of cohesion in today's society. They see an increasing individualization and differentiation as in part due to large flows of migrations and their associated multicultural and multiethnic configurations. Religion has lost its binding function in society; comprehensive ideologies are discredited. Religion is no longer a dominant principle for organizing sport clubs in the Netherlands. Those clubs that are still organized along religious lines question their own identity. Various organizations shower the citizen with immense amounts of often contradictory information or disinformation. Information is interwoven with temptation and deception. All this could lead to a society of calculating citizens who only wish to maximize their own interests, who intend to exploit services to their own advantage, who act as consumers or as people in need of care instead of accepting an active responsibility within and for society. Such citizens could endanger welfare arrangements. This threatens democracy, the constitutional state and the welfare state. Members of the Dutch government (from those leaning toward the left to those leaning toward the right) are united in their appeal for communal spirit and for shared norms and fundamental values. They see politics as a moral enterprise or, in other words, as having a social directive function in order to influence norms and values (de Ruijter, 1995).

Integrative view: Cohesion based on consensus

All those who appeal to citizens to develop and embrace a shared pattern of standards and values as a necessary condition for modern society, find themselves, perhaps unwittingly, in a classical sociological tradition. They follow in the footsteps of, among others, Emile Durkheim. In his study *De la division du travail social* (1893), which was published over 100 years ago, he referred to the increasing dangers of the decay of moral principles (anomie) because of increasing differentiation and individualization. Differentiation and individualization were seen as consequences of an increasing division of labor due to industrialization. Durkheim argued that the cohesion of society is based on the solidarity between members of society. It is not a matter of violence or of repression, but of a moral order. Feelings of social interdependence have become subordinate to mutual economic dependence in modern society, with its extensive division of labor.

Yet Durkheim realized that mutual dependence does not create solidarity overnight because interdependency also can result in feelings of resentment. Contractual relations that are the result of specialization and the division of labor for example, are ultimately grounded in moral values. Observing a contract is an obligation. When this moral obligation has not been internalized as a norm, strife instead of solidarity is the result. Consequently, common notions, representations and a corresponding morality are deemed to be very important to the functioning of society. People have to be educated and trained in this. This has become especially problematical today because the belief in religious sanctions has disappeared and comprehensive political ideologies have fallen into discredit, and, because of large migration flows and the accompanying multicultural and multiethnic configurations. This places additional demands on education to include moral education and on a strongly developed sense of solidarity with the community (one's native country).

In this view society will disintegrate if its members are not strung almost like beads on a string of common motives, cognitions and values. Plural society is perceived to function adequately only if there is a consensus about fundamental values and norms among the various groups in society. It is assumed that without a basis of like-mindedness, diversity will cause a society to disintegrate. Although there is room for limited variations on the same basic theme, unity requires one group to make the other into a replica of itself through socialization processes. The adherents of the integrative view usually concentrate on the control of reproduction mechanisms (de Ruijter, 1995).

Critique of the integration perspective

We propose three arguments for the rejection of integrative thinking.

Plurality

An appeal to communal spirit and for shared (fundamental) values and norms is understandable, but cannot work in the pluralistic society of this day and age. Pluralism has obtained a more central position and has become more problematical than integrationists realize. In the past, society could be mapped and approached by its segments and groups. This is much less the case today. The view that the central values of citizenship (communal spirit, responsibility and political commitment) are transferred through churches, unions and schools is no longer tenable in an absolute sense. Different ideologies and practices are being constructed in a multitude of various societal forms. People create their own distinctive signs of recognition and symbols, make new rules and models, and form identities through processes of inclusion and exclusion. There is a plurality of normative orientations and an increasing international orientation.

Unpredictability

The increasing cultural multiformity and individualization make the course of social processes less predictable. Nobody has sufficient and up to date knowledge of the changes that are currently taking place. Control based on knowledge - the ideal of Enlightenment - has therefore become problematic. According to van Gunsteren (1992) this is The Unknown Society. From the viewpoint of administrators, society has become less recognizable than it was thirty years ago. The Unknown Society, unsettles existing schemes of representation. Categories, data and institutions, which are used to represent social reality, turn out to be repeatedly unreliable. Are political parties representative? Are the data files correct? Are the social partners able to hold on to their employees? What is a family? What is an ethnic minority? If (democratic) representation seems to fail, some politicians try to improve it: through ad hoc corrections, by going to the people and listening to them, by attempting repeatedly again to develop a system guaranteed to bridge the gap between representation and the represented in the future. Obviously society behaves differently now than was expected. It seems impossible to adjust current conceptual schemes to incorporate these changes. An additional complicating factor is the increasing resistance against uniform rules and solutions.

The state may want uniformity but cannot object against the obscure nature of plurality, since the democratic constitutional state explicitly allows this, and even stimulates it. It cannot solve control problems that are the result of the increase in diversity and in a lack of knowledge about society by modeling the required behavior of citizens. The state cannot impose behaviors that are in accordance with the system (observance of rules, willingness to sacrifice oneself, political participation) in the name of citizenship. After all, this appeal is paradoxical: it tells free citizens how they should behave. Citizenship, however, implies the autonomy of citizens, the freedom to judge for oneself, to not participate and to be uninterested (van Gunsteren 1992)

Cognitive and normative diversity

Not only does the integrative appeal not work, it is also superfluous. Communication in a society does not require its citizens to have the same cognitions, standards and values. Participants in a stable socio-cultural system do not have to have the same map of that system to select the expected behavior under the different relevant conditions. Cognitive and normative diversity is the rule rather than the exception, even in so-called primitive closed societies. Yet these systems remain intact. Therefore it would be appropriate to describe culture as an instrument or vehicle to organize diversity (de Ruijter, 1995).

Cohesion based on coordination

From a coordinative view, a culture or society is not a system of common codes, but an implicit contract with respect to a diversity in expectations regarding behavior (Wallace, 1962). Living together minimally consists of at least two interacting parties carrying out mutually related actions. The chain of actions may be the result of different views and action strategies of the participants. However, the ability to anticipate the behavior of the other is of primary importance. It does not matter whether these expectations are based on an incorrect idea about the cognitions pertaining to other practices. Cognitive diversity may even be a condition for processes to take place in an adequate and successful way in society. Not only will different practices become dysfunctional in a society if the participants have a comprehensive common knowledge about each other, but hidden agendas will become very small. The non-sharing of common knowledge also allows the creation of a more complex system than most participants can grasp, as Wallace (1962) already argued convincingly more than 30 years ago (see also Sperber and Wilson, 1986).

In this option culture is a data processing mechanism that functions by means of actions or practices that are conducted according to certain rules or discourses. The nature and effect of the rules or discourses have not been determined in advance: They themselves are constituted as practices (Verweel, chapter 1 in this book). Furthermore, the process of solidification is infinite. The rules or discourses are constantly being developed. Rules, explicit or implicit guidelines to behave in a certain way, function on five different levels. A person who is going to participate may - before or during this action - (a) take note of the relevant rules, (b) come to understand these rules, (c) believe in these rules, (d) act according to these rules, (e) internalize these rules (see Spiro, 1966; Spradley, 1972). The development and continuation of patterns of action do not necessarily require the completion of all five levels. The concrete daily practice is the basis. Many rules may be of an implicit and tacit nature because they are 'learned' through participation and experience, not through explicit instruction.

Rules or discourses are also recursive. A person can generate and interpret a potentially infinite set of cultural actions or practices through only a limited number of rules. This feature of rules also enables an individual to anticipate the - previously unknown - behavior of others. In other words, people are active as actors, involved in constantly creating and recreating significance. The actions that people carry out in this context are often not equivocal, bound or stable, but only direct the attention, 'merely' point out, focus, mobilize or imply. They do however, impose some structure on experience by placing the latter in a context. The context is a socio-psychological construction, part of the total of assumptions individuals have about the world. In this sense context is not limited to information about the immediate material and social environment. Each context is embedded in a more comprehensive context. There are no boundaries to 'context.'. Although it is possible to draw a line that marks the boundaries, it will only be a temporary one. Individuals construct contexts, and modify them, based on experiences throughout their lives. The world can best be seen as a continuous flow of events, rather than as consisting of many simple constant and static structures.

Globalization and localization

This world or transnational system, with its own laws and rules, goes hand in hand with growth of mutual dependencies and a condensation of relationships and interactions between increasingly more actors (see for example Appadurai 1990; Wallerstein, 1975). This is illustrated by the growth in the number of football matches, the creation of a European League and the search by those in other sports, including korfball, for globalization by holding a WK in India. Standardized time, money and expert systems are introduced everywhere. A massive, global exchange of people, goods, services and images is made possible by telecommunication and transport technology. This may result for example, in television producers deciding the time at which football matches are played or marathons are run.

The migration across long distances is characterized by a rapid increase and a greater potential for distribution of goods and services; increasingly more countries and regions are becoming involved in networks which span the globe. Often lifestyles, consumption patterns and other forms of cultural expression are exchanged across an increasing number of locations. Michael Jordan, the basketball star, is as well known in the Netherlands as in the USA because of advertising (Nike - air). Developments of a political, ideological, religious or cultural nature connected to a specific region, culture or period are being echoed in large parts of the world.

The rate of globalization is visible in all domains of life: the scale of intercontinental migration, the mass international tourism, the spreading of new single issue social movements and ideologies, the $300 billion transacted across nations daily in 1995, etc. Gaps between some sectors of society are increasing. In a period of 'open borders', of advanced specialization and division of labor, and, of continually increasing physical and socio-cultural mobility, society is becoming more pulled apart than has ever been the case (Salet, 1996).

Social agents (people, organizations, governments) can rely less and less on the power of what already exists. The nation state is being transformed as emphases shift to above or below-state arrangements. There is a transfer of formal state powers to continental 'power blocks', with, at the same time, a steady increase in regulations at regional and local levels. 'The most obvious reasons for this change [in globalization] were the growing capital intensity of manufacture;

31

the accelerating momentum of technologies; the emergence of a growing body of universal users; and, the spreading of neo-protectionist pressures' (Brenner, 1996, p.19). A new market structure has arisen; important multinationals became global concerns. Nike, for example, is a transnational company that sponsors athletes. Are those athletes 'working' for their own country or for Nike when competing in the Olympic Games? What if Adidas sponsors the national team? This globalization not only refers to processes but also means that the world as a whole is adopting systemic properties in which characteristics of each particular entity have to be understood within the framework of the world as a whole (e.g. Robertson 1992, Friedman 1995). 'In short, a world wide web of interdependencies has been spun, and not just on Internet' (de Ruijter 1997, p.382).

Interestingly, the increasing globalization creates favorable conditions for all sorts of forms of particularization, localization and even fragmentation (see for example, Friedman, 1995; Giddens, 1990; Hannerz, 1992; Latour, 1994; Robertson, 1992, 1995). Globalization includes an export of institutions that create specific conditions for social practice. Most of the rights to televise the Olympic Games are bought by American television companies. It is their (American) interpretation of sport that is seen all over the world. Kenyan athletes who excel in athletics sometimes get scholarships to universities in the United States. To what extent do their experiences within the American sport structure interact with Kenyan constructions of gender and race/ethnicity?

Responses to global instability, however, can also serve as a reaffirmation of local orthodoxies. Transmigrants act, take decisions and develop identities while embedded in networks of relationships that bind them with two or more nation states simultaneously. They give new meanings to social practices/discourses/rules when situated in a different context. Immigrants, for example, are sometimes stricter in the following of religious rules in their 'new' country than they were in the country of origin. They develop new spheres of experiences and new kinds of social relations creating a situation of 'in-betweenness' and resulting in the hybridization of institutions, and the particularization, sometimes even fragmentation of world views and moral frames of reference (Baumann, 1990). Individuals and groups, confronted with the uprooting of many existing local identities, feel an increasing need to construe or invent' new identities.

The emergence of a transnational system implies the rebirth of nationalism, regionalism and ethnicity. This means for example that Kenyans compete for their country after training abroad. In other words, globalization cannot exist without its corollary, the processes of localization (Hannerz 1992; Boessenkool & van Eekeren, chapter 7 in this book). Apparently processes of globalization and localization constitute and stimulate each other. In this era of time-space compression, distant localities are linked so that local happenings are shaped by events occurring many miles away and vice versa (Giddens, 1990). Although geographical ties of identities have become less 'natural' because of globalization processes - it is a case of 'de-territorialisation of identities' (Malkki 1992) - people cling to a geographical grid for the construction and experiencing of a cultural or ethnic identity.

These 're-inventions of tradition' (Roosens 1989) can partly be interpreted as a new defensive orthodoxy, in which - paradoxically - the modern communication technology is intensively used. As a result some group borders fade, but others are more strongly articulated and defended. Various (corporate) agents, with their divergent histories, views and interests, are thus engaged in ongoing negotiations to define reality and to obtain access to scarce resources. Within these 'exchanges and negotiations of meaning', the various identities are expressed, affirmed, commented on, externally imposed and adjusted in mutual relationships. Individuals and groups thus have multiple identities. An athlete for example, who is a member of an Italian professional team may end up competing against her teammates while she plays for the Dutch national team against Italy. Multiple identities lead to diversity and ambiguity and result in a decrease in the acceptability of the certainties offered by local or national communities with their concomitant moral orientations. The resulting plurality of 'representations' and 'voices' produces conflicts, controversies and variations, but also to attempts to live peacefully together, to coordinate activities, and to balance interests (see for example the friendship between Carambeau (French) and Seedorf (Dutch) when they were reunited by playing for Real Madrid (Spain) after an Italian adventure; the struggle between Davids (the Netherlands) and Seedorf (Netherlands) in the final of European Cup between Real Madrid and Juventus.) In short, presently society is 'nothing but' a never ending story of antagonistic cooperation within the constraints of the ongoing dialectical processes of globalization and localization.

Both approaches to cohesion are tied to the ongoing discussion about the development of the nature of society in terms of globalization and localization. Our daily lives are governed by products and images originating from all the corners of the world. We can justifiably and reasonably speak of globalization. This not only concerns the incorporation of increasingly more people in an encompassing political economic system. Globalization refers also to socio-cultural homogenization processes. We see the world turning into a global village (McLuhan 1964). Although this process has been going on at least since the end of the Middle Ages, we have to acknowledge that the current globalization wave is rather unique in scope and impact. This is usually interpreted positively, if not in terms of modernization.

Perhaps there is a break in this trend now that we are at the beginning of a new millennium. The modernization of the world is increasingly called into question. Is this 'uniformization' of the world already a fact? Is homogenization an ideal or a nightmare? Some of us applaud the increase in diversity as a source of models for alternate behaviors or as the empowerment of indigenous peoples and marginalized groups. Others regret this diversity by pointing to the growing complexity and uncertainty of our existence. Although evaluating this diversity is problematic, we cannot, however, escape it. We must live in a reality characterized by this diversity. The complexity connected to the diversity is inevitable and will perhaps increase due to the interrelatedness of globalization and localization processes. The product of the interaction between these two extremes can be interpreted as hybridization (Latour 1994) and is closely aligned with fragmentation.

The relationship between society and organizations

Society supplies a broad context of institutions, social and legal systems, people and meanings for sport organizations. We recognize demographic, social-cultural, political and economic discourses, sectors and institutions. They form a structure that provides the conditions in which change and continuity can take place for each sector and the organizations that operate within it. Societal tendencies towards globalization and localization shape not only the context for sport organizations, but directly and indirectly influence the assignment of meaning in sport organizations. When people deal with situations in sport organizations, they use these ideas (directly) to give meaning to their experiences. The influence of societal tendencies is indirect because the necessary conditions, including societal legitimation and financing of sport clubs by societal administrators (civil servants and politicians), are interpreted considering these developments.

The relationship between society and sport develops through interactions and the assignment of meaning; the meanings created within the club are related to the possibilities the meanings have in the various arenas (organization and society). This refers primarily to those who are actively involved in sport since the scope of the interaction is limited by the requirement to be a member. Of course, there are many who are passively involved as spectators, fans, etc. who also assign meanings to sport. We, however focus primarily on the interaction between societal and sport specific meanings in the context of organized sport using the sport club as the organizational setting.

The boundaries between organizations and society are fluid because both society and (sport) organizations are dynamic. Resources, meanings and people continually cross these boundaries. The uniqueness of an organization is determined by the specific mechanisms of inclusion and exclusion that operate at an intersection of various processes. The adding of a new idea to the sport setting, such as 'market economy', leads to a new understanding of the idea 'market economy'; simultaneously the introduction of the concept 'market economy' begins to change the specific configuration of the structure and culture of the (sport) organization itself (Anthonissen, chapter 4 in this book). This is what we mean when we say the organization is 'half open.' The societal context does not totally dominate nor determine the sport organization. In addition, the sport organization also influences its context. Weick (1995) calls this an enacted environment. Those in (sport) organizations produce part of the context by the way they experience and define the situation.

The diversity in meanings assigned by outsiders and insiders has to be coordinated with each other. The processes of globalization and localization described in this chapter mean, for example, that there is a greater diversity in meanings attributed to societal qualities such as competition, persistence, teamwork, etc. which are supposedly developed in sport. Sport organizations therefore, have the task of incorporating diversity in external and internal processes of communication through consensus or the coordination of differences and thus establishing a form of social cohesion in the sport club.

Developments and changes

The legal rules, social discourses and structures of sport organizations are also threatened by the search for external legitimization. Many sports associations are facing divergent dilemmas such as a decrease in membership, lack of management support, financial shortages, etc. (see for example, Anthonissen and Boessenkool, 1996). Individuals must find their way through many possibilities. Those who live in Utrecht, for example, can choose from among 300 sport clubs but how do you choose the 'best' one? The result is plurality, different opinions, ambiguity and the development of many cultures. Individuals (read: members) and organizations (read: sport clubs) are faced with the question: who or what are we? The answers to this question are becoming increasingly diverse and variable. The possibilities from which to choose, continue to increase in number Careers, memberships, ties, and loyalties are less stable, less predictable, and less standardized than they were in past decades. Membership in and lifelong loyalty to the district or church-related sport club are no longer automatic.

The increase in choices is not necessarily positive or negative. The break from traditional ties has given individuals new possibilities to interpret their lives according to their own insights and choices. Smothering forces that rob people of their initiative and mobility, have partially fallen by the wayside. At the same time, however, the unequal distribution of power and the (lack of) availability of resources also has resulted in a more uneven distribution of those possibilities. A certain erosion of community ties is occurring. Some sports clubs and associations are becoming stronger and more professional while others are weakening and even disappearing altogether (see for example Boessenkool, chapter 5 in this book). Certain sports are threatened with becoming marginal because they are not commercially attractive.

Sports clubs often find themselves in a kind of 'prisoner's dilemma'. On the one hand, a process of individualization is taking place in which the wishes and demands of the members are interpreted differently (sometimes wrongly defined as 'consumerism'). On the other hand, a process of economizing is taking place that allows market demands and relies on rationalization and bureaucratization. Under the influence of both processes, sport associations change from being moral communities to being contract communities. This process is beautifully described by an administrator of a cycling association as going from ' a beer can coaster to floppy disk'. The differences are all too well known by every sport administrator; they are visible in a decrease in involvement (often the complaint of the former manager who still, after many years, devotes 30 hours a week to 'his club') and the introduction of market models copied from trade and industry by 'younger' managers.

The key question, naturally, is how sports associations and in particular their managers, will deal with this dramatic increase in diversity. Currently, administrators and managers seem to react in the same way. Their ideal solution consists of converting their sport club to a professional sport organization characterized by a market orientation and professionalism. The wish (or dream, perhaps) of dozens of amateur soccer clubs is to be able to play at least at the second class level of the Royal Dutch Football Association (KNVB). Administrators think this level can be reached if they get sponsors, offer VIP boxes, establish foundations supporting the top level team, attract and pay players, etc. This way of thinking, however, ignores the fact that the frame of reference for the traditional sport club is still partly controlled by such internally oriented values such as participation and solidarity. The desired 'professional' organization is totally at odds with these values. Professional organizations are characterized by quality, efficiency, effectiveness and orientation to the environment (Rubingh & Westerbeek, 1992). We have strong doubts whether this increasingly common way of dealing with the observed dilemmas is the right way. We doubt that many administrators can do justice to each of these orientations within their sport clubs. We believe that the nature and meaning of both forces have scarcely begun to dawn on these sport managers.

Sport organizations

We define the organization as a dynamic intersection of processes of inclusion and exclusion that are assigned meanings by actors through formal and informal interactions. The relationships between actors and the social structure (intersections), the process of making sense or assigning meaning and the multilayered (formal and informal) aspects of the organization all play a role. Specifically, actors engage in sense making by bringing together, synthesizing and extending their meanings from their personal, societal and organizational worlds. Thus, a variety of systems of meaning are often active in an organization. Three approaches — integration (systems model), differentiation (groups model) and fragmentation — explained and discussed by Verweel (chapter 1 in this book), are often used to help make sense of these dynamic interactions. We assume that these different models interact and produce each other. If the characteristics of each group evoke each other (the 'Other') then that means that the organization is characterized by several paradoxical movements: self interest versus organizational interest; organizational culture versus subcultures; team work versus competition; centralized authority versus coalitions of power; clarity versus complexity and ambiguity, etc. Organizational life is dominated not so much by differences in sense making but by the tensions evoked by the aforementioned forces that act simultaneously. Social cohesion is reinforced and shaped by the interacting forces that stimulate unity and diversity.

The metaphor of the theater is apt (see also Bailey, 1977). The actors are on stage acting out the roles using agreed upon rules and places on the stage including entering and leaving the stage. The script requires that 'John' be addressed as the chair after the opening and that a 'lie' is described as something that is 'not totally based on the facts interpretation of reality.' The prescribed performance makes it possible to evaluate the behaviors of the actors. The public sees the performance on stage but the performance is only possible because of what plays behind the scenes. The public knows that actions occur behind the scenes or in the wings but not what. This is part of the unspoken agreement between the public and the actors and makes it possible for some actors to play more than one role. The wings are directly connected to the stage and it is there that most of the preparations take place; it is the place where self interests and meanings are worked out so that the roles can be played in an agreed upon manner. The dressing room, however, is another level. It is a place where one can be 'out of role' and where there is room for personal reflection. The actors can see each other or themselves (in the mirror) again as individuals when they are scrubbed clean after the performance.

The described rationality of the roles dominates the stage without diminishing the subjective (own interpretation of the role) and the intersubjective (the spark that fans out to the other actors and the public). The individual and interpersonal self, based on self reflection and confidence, dominates in the dressing room but without the objective whole of the performance falling away. Formal positions do influence communication. The interests of the play and of the players dominate. The arena of the (sport) organization also contains these various layers.

Lastly, we wish to make the distinction between the primary and the supportive process. Actual participation in sport is the primary process. The sport club and the sport associations provide the supporting controlling and administrative structure and the place where the social ties between players are expressed (along the side lines and in the restaurant). We distinguish between the social and the organizational functional elements in the supporting structure and in sport itself. The functional elements such as skill techniques, strategies, personal condition, concentration, etc. and the social interactions among people are important. A football player is a person with thoughts and emotions at the same time that he or she is the lazy wing with fluid movements and a shot that is difficult to stop. Yet this wing is like the actors in the previous paragraph. We expect the wing to carry out the requirements of the position (objectified role) and to adapt his or her technical skills to the play. Personal thoughts and emotions must be kept subordinate to the execution of the play/game.

Conclusion: Cohesion in sport and society

Sport and society are both subjected to drastic changes that ask for interpretation (making sense). Both involve changes interpreted by sport managers as a loss: a loss of social ties, a loss of certainty, a loss of a future in which you could count on agreement in meaning and in shared experiences. We have described frameworks that include both sport and society to enable analyses and offer directions for solutions. Individuals in society and in their (sport) organizations must continually negotiate between self and group interests, between consensus and dissent, between team work and competition, between individuality and group identity. Individuals take the meanings that come forward in areas of their lives such as sport participation. They synthesize and arrange these meanings and in interaction with others, (re)constructs them to make sense of their experiences. We shall examine the construction of meanings in interactions and practices in the following chapters.

Annelies Knoppers

Gender and [sport] organizations

Overview

According to many statistics the emancipation of women is almost complete. There is no occupation that is completely sex segregated anymore except perhaps that of priest in the Roman Catholic church. Advertisements for jobs now usually say that both men and women are welcome to apply. In previously all male areas such as politics, engineering and the armed forces, the percentage of women is increasing. Whereas the Olympic Games in 1896 consisted only of male participants, one hundred years later, 36% of the participants were women (Andrews, 1998). The International Olympic Committee once an all male committee, now includes a few women members. These changes have not just been confined to women. Men are entering previously all-female occupations such as nursing. The number of hours men devote to household and child-rearing tasks has increased. Thus it may seem that we need to pay little attention to the emancipation of women and subsequently, to the topic of gender and organizations.

There are however statistics about the emancipation of women in European countries that reveal a different picture (Dossier, 1999). The percentage of women in the labor force ranges from a low of 36% in Spain to a high of 48% in Sweden; the percentage of directors and managers who are women ranges from a low of 9% in France to 53% in Italy; the incomes of women compared to that of men range from 30% in Spain to 45% in Sweden (Niphuis-Nell, 1997). Women still spend almost twice as much time on care-related tasks than men do. Dutch women and men with paid work, for example, spend respectively 16.4 hours and 8.4 hours per week on tasks related to the home (Equality, 1999).

The situation in sport is not that much different and does not vary much among countries in the Western world. All sport - related areas such as participation, leadership, management, publicity and organizations, were once the domain of men. Now women and men participate in sport in equal numbers in sport yet the statistics about leadership and management are skewed. In the Nether-lands, for example, only half of all the sport participants are men and yet 82 -89% of the coaches and 91% of the board members are men (Emancipatieraad, 1997; Stol, 1995). In Canada half the entry level jobs in sport organizations are held by men yet men comprise three quarters of the executive directors and 90% of the national coaches (Hall et al., 1990). In the early 1970s, 8% of the college coaching positions of women's teams in the USA were occupied by men; now that percentage is 52%; This statistic could be an example of achieving gender equity was it not for the statistic that 98% of the collegiate men's teams are coached by men (Acosta & Carpenter, 1998; Coakley, 1998). Hargreaves (1994) reports an increase in the percent of women participating in sport <u>and</u> in the proportion of men in leadership positions in sport in Britain. Although women occupy as many entry level positions in sport as do men, there are imbalances in the gender ratio in leadership positions. In other words, the emancipation of women and their entry into sport has meant relatively more jobs for men than for women. Obviously there are dynamics underlying these trends that need to be explored.

In the 1980s the most commonly used approach to deal with this issue was to determine what women needed to 'learn' to advance to higher positions in (sport) organizations (for a discussion of this approach, see Knoppers, 1987). The question was: 'What do women lack or need to learn to work here?' The answers consisted of activities such as the holding workshops to teach women the necessary skills, targeting the recruitment of women, establishing affirmative action programs, developing mentoring programs etc. These activities may have had a positive impact on individual women but generally, the percentage of women in leadership positions in (sport) organizations remains, and is, low as the earlier cited statistics suggest. In addition, the problem cannot just be located in women because there has also been resistance to the entry of women. Their increasing number (into predominantly male organizations) is seen as bringing 'gender' and 'sexuality' into the organization (Collinson & Hearn, 1994; Hearn & Parkin, 1987; Pringle, 1989). Men complain that now they have to watch their language and to censure their jokes, that women do not have to be as qualified as the men, and, that policies against sexual harassment make them vulnerable (Acker, 1992; Cockburn, 1991; Collinson & Collinson, 1992; Collinson & Hearn, 1994; Hall et al., 1990; Knoppers & Bouman, 1998; Knoppers & Elling, 1999b; McKay, 1993).

Obviously other approaches are called for than those that focus on women only. One such approach explores the way we assign meanings to gender and how these meanings are embedded in organizational discourse and practices. In this chapter I want to explore connections between gender and organizations using the relational perspective to gender and the concept of discourse as explained in the introductory chapter of this book. In this chapter I will try to answer two questions.

- What is the dominant discourse about gender in (sport) organizations?

- How have (sport) organizations been gendered and what are the consequences?

My focus will primarily be on men as men. Collectively they have created most of the discourse about organizations to the extent that male-defined discourses have become hegemonic. In addition, they dominate the positions of leadership and are therefore likely to be in the position of 'change agents' (Kanter, 1984) and relatively little attention has been paid to them as gendered beings in the organizational literature.

Organizations: Ideology of meritocracy and discourse of equal opportunity

As has been emphasized repeatedly in this book, organizations are created by actors. Although each organization has its own structure and culture, those structures and cultures are webs of meanings based on daily routines. These routines are 'the practices of actors in organized contexts' (Ramsay & Parker, 1992, pp. 253). Many actors including social theorists see these practices as 'neutral' or at least free from ideologies related to social group relations such as gender, race and ethnicity (for a discussion of this point see for example Acker, 1990; 1992; Benschop, 1996; Calás & Smircich, 1992a,b; Hearn & Parkin, 1983). Consequently much theorizing and practical advice about organizations are in part based on an assumption that organizations are 'free' from gendered meanings. Such theorizing and advice treat everyone (whatever gender and race/ethnicity) similarly. As I alluded to earlier, if there are 'problems', then they are usually located in differences, that is, how women, for example, are different from men.

Another assumption underlying many theories about organizations is that those who hold similar positions or work in the same organization, experience the organization/position in similar ways (Acker, 1992; Collinson & Hearn, 1994; Kanter, 1977). In part this may be true because, especially at higher levels, those selected for positions tend to resemble those already there. These similarities include gender and race/ethnicity. Kanter (1977) calls this 'homologous reproduction.' In other words, most of those who hold upper level positions (i.e. white middle class heterosexual males), feel most comfortable with and tend to select those who are most like themselves. Kanter argues that homologous reproduction is an effort to reduce organizational uncertainty. Homologous reproduction does not mean that women or minorities will not be chosen for upper level positions but means that they have the greatest chance of being selected when they are most like those already there, that is like white middle class heterosexual males. The assumption of ideological neutrality with respect to social relations may rest on the process of homologous reproduction. Yet the work force is becoming increasingly diverse so that homologous reproduction has become a questioned practice. In addition, homologous reproduction may also limit organizations since they function in a context where multiculturalism is a dominant factor. Cultural diversity may strengthen organizations more than does homologous reproduction.

Another assumption often made about organizations is that meritocratic practices prevail, that is, that opportunities for promotion, access to power and to resources are (gender) neutral. For example, in a study of Dutch banks, Benschop (1996) found that the majority of the employees thought that everyone, regardless of gender, had equal opportunity for promotion if they worked hard enough and/or possessed the necessary qualifications.' Meritocracy was assumed to prevail and was perceived to be gender blind. The under-representation of women in high positions was primarily attributed to reasons located in women themselves such as lack of motivation or ability and having child care responsibilities.

In summary then, research about organizations often rests on assumptions of non-gendered meanings, shared experiences and the prevalence of meritocratic processes. These assumptions pertain not only to members of organizations but also to researchers. Hearn & Parkin (1983), in a discussion about gender and organizations, have shown how many scholars make similar assumptions. When such scholars do pay attention to gender then they usually do so by focusing on the under- representation of women in higher positions. They tend to equate gender with women. These assumptions underlie much of the dominant discourses about organizations and about sport and often lead to the conclusion that gender is a 'nonissue.'

Sport organizations: Perceived neutrality

Sport

Many people assume that sport participation is an ideologically -free activity, that sport participants experience their sport similarly (at least within the same sport) and that those experiences are largely independent of social relations such as gender (Coakley, 1998; Hall, 1996). Being a member of the Olympic basketball team for example, is assumed to mean similar things for all the team members such as playing for and being one of the best in your own country. Sport is also often seen as an agent of integration in which boundaries marked by gender and race/ethnicity collapse because sport provides a place for every-one to play together (Coakley, 1998). The visible presence of black and white athletes playing together on one team and the growth of women's sport seem to document the integrative and emancipatory meanings given to sport partici-pation and to confirm the assumption that sport is a neutral activity with re-spect to social group relations. The results of research (Knoppers & Bouman, 1996; 1998) conducted with 720 Dutch coaches in eleven different sports for example, show that most of the coaches felt that anyone who wishes to be-come a coach can do so; they agreed that a policy of meritocracy prevails in the naming of coaches for the higher level women's and men's teams. Only 25% of the coaches felt that affirmative action plans and special programs to recruit women and girls are needed.

Sport organizations

Given the assumption of gender-neutrality that prevails in discourses about sport and about organizations, it is not surprising that a belief in the prevalence of non-gendered meanings, similarity of experiences and the prevalence of meritocratic processes also underlies assumptions about sport organizations. Researchers (Hall et al., 1990; Knoppers, 1992; Knoppers & Bouman, 1998; Macintosh & Whitson, 1990; McKay, 1993), who have conducted research in sport organizations in various countries, unanimously conclude that a main barrier to bringing about change in the ratio of men to women and in the hegemonic male culture in sport is the failure of those in positions of leadership in organizations to see inequality as an issue. These 'leaders' tend to see sport organizations as places of equal opportunity where performance 'erases' skin color and gender and is objectively measured by outcome. When the leaders in the sport world do see gender ratio and a gendered culture as an issue, they frame it as a woman's issue instead of as an issue affecting both women and men and/or the culture of an organization. Sport organizations or clubs, for example, may note that they have too few female participants and therefore actively recruit new female members. Or, if they want more female coaches, they try to talk women, usually mothers of athletes, into becoming coaches. New or potential board members attend workshops or courses to learn to become 'good' and effective board members.

Although programs of recruitment do result in an increase in the number of female athletes, coaches and sport managers, the drop out rate is relatively high (Coakley, 1998; Knoppers & Bouman, 1996; 1998). Coakley (1998) asserts that 'women get jobs only when they present compelling objective evidence of their qualifications, combined with other evidence that they can do things the way successful men have done them in the past' (p. 228). Homologous reproduction is therefore also a characteristic of most sport organizations. In addition, the relatively high drop out rate of women is seen as their problem and is often attributed to women's lack of motivation and knowledge and to unavoidable child care responsibilities (Knoppers & Bouman, 1996; 1998; Knoppers & Elling, 1999b). Hiring men is much easier.

Obviously there are similarities in the dominant discourse about gender in nonsport and sport organizations. It could be argued that the dominant gender discourse might even be stronger in sport organizations because most of those actors involved in giving meaning to organizational practices have a sport background. The dominant organizational and the sport discourses reinforce each other with little room for alternate discourses. There is some statistical evidence from several countries to substantiate the claim that sport organizations are more conservative. Women, for example, occupy fewer positions in Dutch sport organizations (10.3%) than in other voluntary organizations (20.4%) including those associated with leisure activities (Emancipatieraad, 1997). The percentage of women administrators in American and British sport organizations is actually decreasing while in other organizations it is increasing (Acosta & Carpenter, 1998; Hargreaves, 1994).

Perceptions of 'neutrality' in organizations

Alternate or marginalized discourses about (sport) organizations do exist, especially in the scholarly literature and are rooted in a critique of the assumption of gender neutrality. One alternate discourse begins with the assumption that actors themselves are not and cannot be 'neutral.' Actors are male or female, are members of an ethnic group, have race and sexual preference, etc. Actors embed their own histories and social positions with respect to various social relations into organizational practice and discourse, that is, into its structure and culture. Their practices reflect, among other things, how they think and talk about gender, race/ethnicity, age, sexual preference, etc. Their gender logic becomes 'an implicit blueprint for how things are to be arranged to produce an efficiently functioning whole . . . Fundamental to efficient functioning is an abstract, ostensibly gender- neutral worker whose central commitment is to the organization and who has no competing time or emotional obligations, such as those to children and spouses' (Acker, 1995, p. 139). The manner in which actors construct this gender logic is based on prevailing discourses about gender in their organization and in the broader societal context.

Women, people of color and ethnic minorities may experience the organization differently than white heterosexual men because their membership in a social group *positions* them differently in relation to the practices and discourses of an organization. If, for example, the language in a position paper or document of an organization is in the male form (and although the caveat 'this applies to everyone' is made) women must spend time and energy 'translating' it. When does 'he/man' refer to everyone and when does it refer to men literally? Which images does usage of 'he/man' elicit among men? Do they think of women also? In addition, use of he/man makes women invisible. This difference in experience goes beyond language/images. For black employees the company picnic may be a time of negotiating 'white corporate culture' rather than a time of relaxation as it might be for white managers. We live in a society where stereotypes about the 'Other' abound. Those who are defined as the Other must continually reflect on actions of others toward them: 'to what extent does this have to do with me being positioned differently in societal structure as compared to the majority and to what extent does this have to do with me personally'?

The meanings given to social relations such as gender are not only part of (daily) interactions but are embedded in the practices and discourses of the organization. In other words, practices and discourse inform each other. Witz and Savage (1992), in their discussion of organizational forms, argue that 'any common patterns of organizing are due not to any technical, functional imperatives but rather to the common embodiment of particular forms of social and power relations within them. ' (p. 9). The same could be said about sport.

Perception of 'neutrality' in sport

Sport is a cultural practice that explicitly focuses on the body. Part of this practice consists of assigning meaning to sport participation and the competitive body-in-action (competitive physicality). These meanings are often constructed in social situations, are often based on the way sport and the sporting body are (re)presented in the media and often differ from those given by the athletes themselves (Messner, 1988; 1992). The meanings given to competitive physicality have played an important factor in informing our discourses about humans as social persons and especially, how we construct race and gender outside sport. Coakley (1998) has written: '... sports are sites in culture where people formulate and put into action ideas about skin color and cultural heritage that they then carry over into the rest of society ... Sport is unique in the sense that it may even trigger a form of race awareness that makes skin color and certain cultural differences very important to many people' (p. 249; p. 286). The same can be said about gender. The performances of men athletes have been often used to 'prove' that men are stronger and are therefore, superior to women (Hall, 1996; Messner, 1988). Yet the performance of white female athletes may also shatter prevailing stereotypes about women being physically weak. The performances of black men and women athletes may empower people of color and simultaneously confirm dominant discourses about blacks and physicality. In other words, the meanings we give to race and gender and other social relations are linked to meanings we give to competitive physicality, are dynamic and multidimensional due to the intersection of social relations and often, contradictory. Although a multiplicity of meanings or discourses about the athletic body may exist, a few have emerged as dominant as people consciously or subconsciously use (or ignore) sport events as sites for reinforcing or contesting the meanings they give to race and gender. Sport therefore is used in the construction and reconstruction of dominant and alternate notions about gender, gendered athleticism and gender ideologies. These meanings influence the ways we organize sport and sport organizations.

The initial organizational form for modern sport was also based on a discourse that understood only male physicality to be suited for sport (Hargreaves, 1994). This resulted in a singular organizational form, that is, sport was primarily organized for (upper class) men. The dominant discourse about women and sport gradually began to change due in part to competing discourses about health and fitness and the emancipation of women (Cahn, 1994; Hargreaves, 1994). Eventually women were allowed to compete but only in competitions designated for them, including many but not all the Olympic sports/events. The dominant discourse and organizational practices kept [men's] sport in the center. This is a good example of how a dominant discourse (only men can excel in sport) changes to accommodate another discourse (women can also compete) but retains its key elements. Sport is still defined in terms of best performance (Anthonissen, chapter 4 in this book). Since the best men outperform the best women, then the dominant discourse about sport will have men as the norm or starting point. Women are simply added on as a 'sub' or marked category.

In discourses in and about sport, men are the implied actors. Women form a 'sub' category in the organizational practices of sport, as is best illustrated in the language used to mark sport; there is for example, 'football' and 'women's football'. Women are mentioned explicitly only when they are actors. Women's sports are always marked in this way; men's sports are rarely designated as such. In other words, we assume that football players are men unless they are marked as women. This assumption underlies much of the culture in sport organizations and has implications as we shall see further on. Men and men's sports are often seen as not having gender, as value-free and form the norm for organizational practices and discourses. This means, as McKay (1993) argues, that the organizational culture of sporting organizations is governed by regimes of [white] masculinity. These regimes take on various interdependent forms. Acker (1992) argues that organizations are gendered through at least four different practices: 1) production of gender divisions; 2) the creation of symbols, images, etc. that justify and sometimes resist gender divisions; 3) interactions between individuals in multiplicity of forms as they create alliances and exclusions, various levels of hierarchy and policies that create divisions; and, 4) the internal mental work individuals must engage in to reinforce, resist and explain those divisions. These practices are based on the assumption that the job and the worker are gender-neutral and that the worker has no body.

In the following section I will discuss each of these processes and show how they are dominated by meanings embedded in the structure of gender, in particular, in masculinity. I use the concept of 'masculinity' as defined by Connell (1987; 1995). He argues that although there are various forms of masculinity but there is one that is what most men desire to be: a hegemonic masculinity. In the western world this masculinity is associated with white, visibly heterosexual and economically successful men. Other masculinities such as that of black and gay men, Connell calls 'subordinate' and 'marginalized.'

Gender and division of labor

There has been enough research to make it almost a truism to say that organizations (and society itself) employ a sexual division of labor and authority (Witz & Savage, 1992). Women 'clean up' that is, they order the material world by soothing, sustaining, cleaning, tidying and facilitating so that men can work and be a part of organizations. Sport organizations are no exception. Discourses that construct sport organizations assume a certain type of (male) subject supported by a (female) subject, that is they assume that men will have female support at home (Knoppers & Bouman, 1996; 1998). Much of the leisure time of men including their involvement as volunteer coach, board members, athlete, etc., is made possible by the domestic work women do (Macintosh & Whitson, 1990). The men involved in the Third Half, (Verweel, chapter 2 in this book) for example, create football as an activity that has priority (on Saturdays) above everything else. They assume a division of labor (women do the shopping while men play). There are no female voices in the exchange. The amount of work women may have had to do to enable these men to play a game of football and to spend time replaying it is not visible in this exchange. Often it is taken for granted. Instead, they speak negatively about a man who does go shopping.

Often men involved in organizations and/or sport fail or refuse to recognize the extent to which their involvement or work is made possible by women's 'domestic' work. This lack of recognition has a broad impact because these men also often occupy positions in (sport) organizations where decisions about child care, about defining a coach's responsibilities, etc., are made. As Reskin (1988) argues 'the dominant groups remain privileged because they write the rules and the rules they write, enable them to continue to write the rules' (p. 60). [Sport] organizations therefore tend to have a gendered structure that assumes that 'work and leisure' are separate from [domestic] life and ignore the interdependence between paid/volunteer work and domestic work (Boyle & McKay, 1995; Connell, 1987). Male coaches, for example, often attribute the lack of women coaches in part to the domestic responsibilities women have but are oblivious to the fact that they as men are able to be active in sport organizations because they have a supportive female partner who takes on the bulk of *their* domestic work (Knoppers & Bouman, 1998). Of course there are men who do recognize the interdependence; these tend to be men who are married to women who have a long history of being involved in sport. (Knoppers & Bouman, 1996).

The relative invisibility of women is not the only way division of labor is embedded in organizational practice however. Women are not totally excluded from organizational life. Gendered divisions of labor are also embedded in positions in organizations. Women and men tend to do different jobs in organizations with more women in lower status positions and more men in higher status positions. Most women working in sport organizations are involved in keeping records, doing secretarial tasks while men occupy positions defined as requiring leadership, administrative duties and ability to work with and generate finances (Hall, Cullen & Slack, (1990). The gender ratio in leadership positions varies from sport to sport and is the most skewed in Dutch football, where despite affirmative action and recruiting programs, 79 women and 10,000 men were certified to coach in 1995 (Stol, 1995). Regardless of type of sport, women coaches are more likely to coach youth, women and lower skilled teams (Knoppers & Bouman, 1996; 1998). Men tend to be the national coaches of both women's and men's teams and head coaches at sport clubs (Emancipatieraad, 1997). Men also numerically dominate sport manager positions at the local, regional and national level in all sport federations (Emancipatieraad, 1997). A similar pattern exists in other Western countries (Coakley, 1998). This division of labor or segregation based on gender strengthens the discourse that associates men with sporting excellence and (organizational) leadership.

Abstract meanings/ creation of symbols

These divisions of labor are continually (re)produced because they rely on abstract images we create about who (type of person) is best suited for a position (Acker, 1992). Leidner (1991) looked at the way meanings were given to positions in which the essential tasks were similar, that is, selling something that consumers do not need. She studied the way those who work in fast food establishments and those who sell insurance were taught to 'sell.' Both jobs require the employees to be pleasant and to accommodate the customer at all times. This type of interaction is usually associated with women. It is no wonder that most of the sales staff in fast food establishments are females. Those involved in the selling of insurance were taught that this 'deference' is calculated, that the seller is really in control; not reacting to verbal abuse did not mean passivity but was defined as a way of not letting the customer take control. It is not surprising then that most of those who sell insurance are men. When positions, paid or unpaid, are created or are vacant, we have images about who should fill those positions. When we think of the chair of the board then we may think 'business man' or 'top football player turned businessman'. When we need a coach for the men's team, we think 'top male athlete'. Images about coaching and other forms of leadership in sports tend to be seen "in terms that are consistent with traditional ideas about masculinity: if you 'coach like a girl' you are doing it wrong; if you 'lead like a man, ' you are doing it right (Coakley, 1998, p. 228).

The equation of sport with men is based on the construction of images through discourses and (re)produced by the media. In a study of materials produced by the Dutch football federation (including the monthly membership magazine), Knoppers & Elling (1999b) found that the dominant image was that of (white) males. In a study of 16 days of sport programming on public television, Knoppers & Elling (1999a) found that 97% of the coverage was devoted to men's sports. This predominance of male images reinforces the idea that sport is about men and that (almost all) males will know more about sport than females. Yet sport does not celebrate all males. It celebrates a certain type of masculinity characterized by strength, individualism, and a visible heterosexuality. These characteristics are part of what Connell (1987; 1995) calls hegemonic masculinity that is an idealized form of what most men want to be like. A gay masculinity for example, is invisible and not celebrated in national sports such as football.

The abstract images that help produce gendered organizations are not just those depicting organizational positions but pertain to all the images and symbols used in an organization ranging from characterizing the organization as a 'family' to using male performance as the norm. Collinson & Hearn (1994) show for example, how the current trend in the scholarly literature emphasizes 'corporate leaders' who have a strong responsibility for managing meaning 'Yet [these] charismatic leadership styles and the establishment of strong corporate cultures often draw upon the gendered imagery of the organization as a family . . . the inherent masculinity of this discourse is rarely addressed . . . (p. 4)

Similarly when we define sport primarily in terms of quantified 'best performance' and limit what counts as sport to those activities where men excel as what matters, the performance of men becomes the abstract standard. Women's bodies are given meanings that make them inferior to men's bodies and that makes inequity in terms of programs and resources seem justified (Lorber, 1993). Those who determine the amount of space given to women's sport in the media often justify the paucity of space by arguing that the media are gender neutral and present only 'best' performance. Women will receive as much coverage as men when they are as good as men (Expert meeting, 1998). Similarly, men's tennis, for example, receives more visibility and more financial rewards because of its relatively greater display of physical power than women's tennis that relies relatively less on power but more on variation greater and longer rallies. Why are 'power' games' and short games defined as 'better' and deserving more attention and financial rewards than 'variety/longer rallies'?

Transforming meanings through interaction

The images, and the value assigned to them, do not exist in themselves but are given meaning in interactive processes between people (Verweel, chapter 1 in this book). Individuals use interactions to create alliances and exclusions, to reinforce or contest various levels of hierarchy, and to create policies that reinforce or erase gendered divisions (Acker, 1992). The process of creating and using networks is a good example of this interactive process. The old boys' network is an informal way through which valuable information is passed along to 'members.' Research on how Dutch coaches got their first and current positions, for example, shows that the majority was asked by current club council members or trainers of whom 80% were male (Knoppers & Bouman, 1996; 1998). Only 5% of the coaches found out about their position through formal advertisements. Since the old boys' network is informal, an aspiring coach cannot apply to join but instead has to have the right contacts, mentors and sponsors to be a beneficiary of the network. This means that anyone who has few, if any, contacts within the old boys' network, has relatively little chance of hearing about and/or obtaining a position. In addition, these networks also often run along the lines of men's teams. X knows Y because they have played together on a team. 'Like seeks like' in other words, homologous reproduction. Unless a sustained effort is made to make a network diverse, a network tends to be exclusive. When networks are organized more formally or when positions are broadly advertised, more women and minorities tend to be members or apply. Women, ethnic minorities and people of color are often shut out because old boys' networks tend to be homogeneous and homo-social. Minorities and women have therefore, often built their own networks but these networks usually do not have the access to people in positions of power as the old boys' network does.

It is through interactive processes such as networks, that individuals give meaning to gender. The Third Half, the exchange between men football players in chapter 2 of this book, is constructed as a time of male bonding that has priority over shopping (with a woman), for example. Tony's wife is sick but the men are more concerned about Tony being part of the team than they are concerned about how she is doing. The team comes before everything. The heterosexual culture of football (and related old boys' networks) is so strong that men can prefer to be with men instead of women and not be thought gay. The same is true of old boys' networks. The dialogue in the Third Half is not just an example of men engaging in male bonding however; it provides examples of men giving meaning to masculinity in interaction with each other. This is not to say that only men 'do' gender when they get together. When women get together they also 'do' gender and construct a 'femininity. When men create a hegemonic masculinity however, that masculinity tends to have greater value in society in general than marginalized masculinities and femininities.

In the Third Half the men athletes criticize each other, make fun of the mistakes and of the men who made them including the referee and an opponent. Connell (1987; 1995) , in his theory about the structure of hegemonic masculinity, argues that hierarchy is a key characteristic of this structure. There is a preferred masculinity that is hegemonic; there are also marginalized masculinities.

By making fun of the mistakes of their opponents and of each other instead of using praise, these men establish a (temporary) hierarchy where they let the others know *they* know how the game should be played. According to Lorber (1993) 'replaying' the game gives men the chance to compete and win vicariously; sexist jokes establish the boundaries of exclusion.

To sustain hegemonic masculinity, men need to differentiate themselves from other men (hierarchy). This group of men involved in the exchange, differentiates itself from women and from the opponent (and referee). They do not for example, share the Third Half with the opponents and referee, but use the occasion to deride them. Having an opponent unifies men; that is one reason sport plays such an important role in the meanings given to masculinity. In (sport) organizations the opponent can take on different forms such as a competitor, but it can also take forms internal to the organization to keep specific groups out or limit their influence. Men's power in organizations is maintained in part though their identification with each other as men; Collinson & Hearn (1994) argue, for example, that one of the things that often unifies male employees is their opposition to equal opportunity programs. Male bonding therefore gives men the opportunity to give meaning to 'masculinity' through interaction with each other. It is a form of bonding to which more societal power is attached than bonding among marginalized men and women.

Internal mental work/individual meaning

All masculine identities, hegemonic or marginalized are fragile, however and constantly shifting. 'Masculine identities constantly have to be constructed, negotiated and reconstructed in routine social interaction, both in the work place and elsewhere (Collinson & Hearn, 1994, p. 8). Besides the formal and interactive work that occurs in (sport) organizations, individuals put much informal effort into creating and maintaining identities that 'fit' the organization. They engage in internal mental work to construct their understandings of the organization's gendered structure and themselves as gendered beings. This 'identity' work is never ending and is embedded in organizational practices and discourses. It consists for example, of choice of appropriate work, use of language, type of clothing chosen and ways of presenting the self as gendered (Acker, 1992). Being a member of a football club, as the participants in the Third Half are, can be an important part of their identity. Keeping women (and also gay men) out or invisible shores up the identity of many men for whom association with sport has become part of their identity.

Knoppers (1992) has shown that token women are often accepted into a male occupation or organization. There is however a critical point (usually around 30 -40%) when the resistance to women becomes organized or visible. Cockburn (1991) argues that many men associate their identity with their job. When the numbers of women in that job reach a critical point that identification is no longer possible then men resist. In a study of shop floor life in the printing industry, Cockburn (1991) found that these male manual workers associated their masculine identity with technical skills; the increase of women into the work place represented a threat to their masculinity. Consequently they engaged in a great deal of resistance behavior to show women they were not welcome.

Most identity work by men in organizations is relative to hegemonic masculinity, that is, what most men aspire to be (but often cannot be). The culture of most sport organizations 'leaves little space and provides little support for those who see the world from different vantage points than those of the white men who have shaped that culture over many years' (Coakley, 1998; p. 228). Men and women may place themselves in opposition to the masculine culture, feel marginalized by it, strive to display some of the desired characteristics associated with hegemonic masculinity, may be supportive of it, etc. In other words, identities are constantly shifting between identification and differentiation. Men will identify with some men as men and differentiate themselves from others (hierarchy) and from women. Women who strive to comply with the male-defined norms and expectations do identity work that often results in being described as 'manly' ' . . . when women are appointed to leadership positions [in sport], it is usually because they have demonstrated those values and ways of behaving that are essentially masculinist and confrontational.' (Hargreaves, 1994, p. 203).

Change

Obviously doing gender in an organization and the gendering of organizations occur in many ways because the aforementioned processes overlap. Identity work is shaped by interactions with others; the meanings created through these interactions impact the way jobs and work are gendered throughout the organization.

Attention to diversity of meanings should not neglect a focus 'upon the structured asymmetrical relations of power between men and women' (Collinson & Hearn, 1994, p. 10). As Foster (1999) argues, 'some men hold power and privilege over all women, as well as marginalized groups of men, due to the intersections of heterosexism, racism, nationalism and/or economic exploitation' (p. 434). Each of the gendered processes is also influenced by processes where race/ethnicity, social class and other social relations are salient. In addition, the gendering of organizations is not separate from the way gender is given meaning in the family, in education, in relationships, in politics, etc. This means that multi-layered and contextual analyses are required when we explore sense making in organizations. Attention should be paid to the way in which the conflation of (white heterosexual) men with managers, coaches, etc. makes it seem that functions and practices in an organization are nongendered, are meritocratic and result in shared experiences. The final chapter of this book will address the issues involved in bringing about change but first we will look at the meanings assigned to sport and sport organizations in various situations (case studies).

Anton Anthonissen

Professionalization: Sport clubs and the reinforcement of the pyramid structure

'It must be a pyramid . . . if you want the first team of the club to be at the top then you must have a foundation on which to build. Results are most important . . . The A team of the youth should compete at the highest possible level to ensure that you have a foundation on which to build success' (sport manager of KDP).

Overview

In a case study of KDP [2] meaning is assigned to competitive sport in order to keep the club's pyramid structure intact. The ways in which club members and sport managers react and interact, suggest that the discourse about the 'pyramid' is a hegemonic discourse situated in an ideology in which top performance is assumed to take place under equitable conditions. Although all those involved subscribe to this ideology, in daily practice the pyramid is associated with inequitable conditions and with processes of estrangement. The marginalized or alternate discourse emphasizes 'self defined achievement' (as a characteristic of competitive sport) which creates room for differences in the ways in which members interpret their membership and in which the club is organized. Members of football club KDP were observed in various activities of the club over a period of nine months. Interviews were conducted with forty members selected from various categories: Sport managers, committee members, top male players, senior members, youth members (boys and girls), athletes who played indoor football, coaches and trainers. These data were supplemented with data based on a review of the literature (see Anthonissen & Boessenkool, 1998 for the review of literature and a complete description of the methodology and results).

(Top) performance is rooted in a broad base

The quotation at the beginning of this chapter shows that the organizational structure of the club KDP (Power through Performance) is based on the idea of a pyramid. If the top men's team is to do well, the logic goes, then a pyramidal structure is a necessity. 'Football is a competitive sport that requires a high level of play/competition. It is therefore logical that we go in that direction' says a sport manager. Just recently, the council of KDP announced that in the future the emphasis will be on high performance sport. Club members wonder to what extent this is a choice that reflects the membership or the wishes of a few sport managers. The council thinks it is necessary to emphasize high performance football because they are afraid that KDP will deteriorate otherwise. 'If we do not make this choice then our level of achievement will go downhill; then you could probably have fun playing football with each other at a lower level but then no one comes to the clubhouse anymore and boys will not want to come and play here.' By attracting locally well-known football players and creating better conditions that enable top performance, the KDP council tries to stay true to the basic structure of the pyramid, to make the club attractive to the youth members, to increase the involvement of members, and to strengthen their ties to the club.

There are ambivalent feelings among club members towards the pyramidal discourse. Several boys who play for the top team want to be the next Kluivert or Bergkamp: 'When there is more financial support for the best boys, then the big clubs will send their scouts . . . that is good for the whole club and for us.' On the other hand, several talented members of this top team are not that ambitious and sometimes choose to do something else on Saturday. When they go to Disneyland on a Saturday, they keep the reason for their absence a secret from the team.

Older members who play at a lower level do not always agree with the logic used to defend a pyramidal structure: 'I come every Saturday just to kick a ball around and then I see the club going in that direction . . . I just want to have some fun with my friends. I realize that we need youth members to ensure continuity . . . but to tell you the truth, that has always been difficult.' Other members of the lower level teams say that although they do not perform at the top level, they do play well every Saturday by their own standards. Therefore, there should be room for them.

This diversity in meanings assigned to playing football for KDP and to performance suggests that KDP members and sport managers [3] see the gap between meanings assigned to 'top performance' and to 'self defined achievement' in sport as a source of tension within the club. Many members think that the club council is innovative and far sighted but also feel that the sport managers want to score with the accomplishments of the first men's team.

The boys to whom this emphasis on high performance is supposed to appeal, have their own ideas however. 'I want to do fun things as well and do not want to come and practice so often' asserts a player of the B1 team. Members of the girls' teams echo these thoughts. Many youth drop out when they are about 16 years old because, according to them, they have so many other opportunities to fill their leisure time. Often they do not want to play football on Saturday or they want to go out Saturday evening and not compete on Sunday so that they can sleep in. Often, there are difficulties in assigning youth members to teams because some of them want to continue to play together despite skill differences. Many boys and girls also have jobs on Saturday which make it difficult for them to play on that day.

Older club members have their own ideas about the participation of youth members. Some think that their enthusiasm to play football in an organized setting is decreasing. The older members worry about the decrease in the number of boys who move up from youth to adult football. They also detect a change in attitude in these boys. They see a mentality that places a decreasing emphasis on top performance and an increasing preference for a more flexible structure. According to these older members, the influence of sponsors plays a significant role. 'They [boys] have it too easy; they first look to see what is in it for them. They do not put the club first.' Older members often compare the club now with 'how it used to be'. The younger members cannot accept this comparison and see no reason to stay with KDP if the climate or the facilities are bad or if they move. An athlete who is dropping out explains: 'We are going to move to a new neighbourhood that also has a football club . . . then I do not have to travel so far to play.'

Sport managers who are members of the youth committee have a somewhat different perspective about the changes in enthusiasm and performance orientation among the youth. They see that there are still boys who want to play football at a high level with a club although these boys do tend to choose clubs with good facilities. Other sport managers think that the demands placed on these boys are not always realistic and that cultural issues play a role as well. '... we have quite a few 'immigrant' boys playing at the youth level. They usually deliver papers on Saturday, have other jobs or just do not come.'

Channels of communication

Most of the members learned about KDP's switch in emphasis to top performance football from the newspaper. The article reports that the KDP council has chosen to pay most of its attention to the top level men's team because football is a competitive and high performance sport. The club will hire a more expensive trainer to enable the top team to play in the top class of Saturday football of the KNVB in two years time. The article continues to say that this emphasis on top performance does not mean that less attention will be paid to the recreation, girls or indoor football teams. 'It [emphasis on the top teams] may never be at the expense of other groups . . . other teams must also have the opportunity to develop themselves,' says a sport manager. Members of these other teams, however, think that the 'new' emphasis does and will affect their teams negatively. They are unhappy because for a long time already most of the attention of the sport managers has been devoted to the top teams. A sport manager acknowledges that some members think this but counters by arguing that it is easy to react like that. According to him, club loyalty plays a large role in this: 'Feelings of loyalty to the club stop about halfway in the second team; they want to play together as a team and expect that everything is well organized. If it would be better organized at another club like Sportlust then they will play for them.'

There are also members who do not play in the top teams who are loyal to and involved with the club: 'For me it [being a member of KDP] goes beyond my team. I wouldn't want to play football for just any club; that is not enjoyable. I like to come to the clubhouse after a match to drink a beer and to see different people.' Others are primarily loyal to their team but do not see that as a problem because they are also loyal to the system. According to them, everyone should be able to enjoy themselves and that means attention should be paid to teams in all the categories. The debate is obviously very polarized.

'Foundation for Top Level Football' and the 'Business Club'

The sport managers continue on their chosen path and create a Foundation for Top Level Football. The Foundation has to generate money and create conditions to ensure that top level football is actually possible. The KDP council defends this action by using recent and similar developments in other clubs as evidence. 'We agreed to the professionalization of football. It was no longer justifiable to take the costs for the top players out of the general budget. . . We discussed this with sport managers of another big club in the city who have taken similar steps . . . the competition among the clubs is increasing and the KNVB and the local government also promote the idea of big clubs who work in a professional manner.'[4]

Other reasons for setting up a foundation include a concern for the decrease in the number of memberships and in the level of performance, the possibilities presented by the building of a new housing development around the fields of the club and the unsatisfactory performance of the current top team. The latter means that more highly skilled players need to be recruited from outside the club. Little, if any, attention is paid to the possible effect this recruitment might have on the current players. The goal is to ensure that the first team performs at the top level so that new players will be attracted to the club. Ironically, the current players of the first team show little interest in the creation of the Foundation. They are not so much interested in the resulting benefits (free membership, travel, shoes, clothes and care and a nominal bonus of fifteen guilders per point per player or position) as they are concerned about the arrival of new players from other clubs and the selection of the first team for next year. Being a member of the first men's team means everything to several players. If they cannot play in that team then they will leave to play for another club.

Besides creating the Foundation Top Level Football, the sport managers also decide to set up a Business Club. This club is associated with the Foundation. It offers businesses in the neighbourhood the opportunity to promote their product(s) to other companies, suppliers and/or other potential customers in KDP's restaurant /bar. The (paid) memberships of the business club serve as an additional source of income for financing the top teams.

A small group of sport managers has worked to implement this plan 'If you do not watch out, then everyone will have spent the money three times already before a cent has come in; even those who recruit new players are already promising rewards for top performance . . . so we have to be careful.' This informal way of working means that many members are caught by surprise when the idea is implemented. This surprise reveals the gap within the club between the formal decision making process and the informal process used to implement the ideas. Not everyone appreciates this informality, especially those who have learned about the plan by reading the newspaper. A sport manager admits that 'the need to do something was very great but the speed with which this all happened is probably too fast for some.' The plan for setting up the business club and for obtaining sponsors had already been publicized by the group of sport managers before the general membership or executive council had even seen the plans. According to several sport managers this was necessary because the contract with the main sponsor was ending. The need to sustain the enthusiasm of the new sponsor is the main reason given for the speed in carrying out the plan and therefore excluding the general membership from discussing it. 'We had no choice' says a sport manager.

Professionalization: More businesslike and more formal

The sudden choice for the creation of a foundation leads to confusion about the organizational structure of the club. Who is responsible for making and implementing policy? For planning skill development? For the financial aspects of the club? What is the relationship between the sport managers of the football club and that of the foundation? What is the influence of the sponsor? The creation of the business club means that sponsorship and membership are interwoven. While the football club has never been known for its businesslike character, according to many members it is becoming more and more businesslike. Much criticism is ventilated in the bar and locker room. Still members stay silent when they are given the opportunity to formally address the issues. Only 12 members show up for the general membership meeting. 'Ah, they made that choice a long time ago and the general membership meeting is only a formality . . . I do not think my ideas will have any impact.' Other members think the same way: 'There is little clarity in the way in which things have been taken care of . . . they lack the courage to be open and straightforward; I think they are afraid of differences of opinion.'

Although there is considerable opposition, the sport managers are convinced that their decision is the correct one. The football club now has to operate in a 'professional' or businesslike manner to attract a sponsor. Sponsors want to know what happens with their money. The club therefore, must make a long term plan covering several years. The sport managers recognize the movement towards a more businesslike approach but think this cannot be avoided. 'I think the decision making process needs to be more structured; in this day and age you cannot do it any other way.' KDP's trend towards professionalization has, however, a negative impact on the involvement and level of volunteerism of the club's members. The difficulties in finding a sufficient number of coaches and other leaders increase even more since fewer members are willing to take on the responsibilities these positions entail. Consequently, the same people are asked for everything; subsequently they feel taken advantage of and quit. The sport managers accept the minimal involvement of many members and use it as an excuse for not consulting them. 'If members do not want to be involved in the decision making process then you can only expect that the council acts on its own.'

The sport managers do not want the other teams to get the feeling that their membership contributions are paying the travel costs of the top teams. By separating the different sources of income the sport managers hope to diminish the tension between income and expenses and clarify matters. 'I think it can work for the benefit of members of the lower teams; otherwise their membership fee would be increased.'

The members are not so concerned about separate budgets however as they are about the rationale and the concern the council has for the rest of the members. Their concern is about 'attention' which means 'being heard', 'being interested' and having access to adequate resources. 'The last time we played with a ball, which according to me, they had received free when they bought a pound of butter.' In the eyes of many members, the attention paid to recreational sport (which is mentioned in the same breath with girls' and indoor football) is decreasing rapidly. Recreational sport is not even mentioned in the new long term plan. The members who play on the lower teams acknowledge that better performances by the top teams are necessary to rebuild and sustain the pyramid but they also want recognition /attention for their own achievements.

Listening but failing to understand

A variety of changes are occurring within KDP that have a major impact on the club. Anthonissen & Boessenkool (1998) have shown that these developments are not unique to the football club KDP, or team sports and that they also occur in the individual sports. Sport managers continue to insist on the traditional relationship between a high level of achievement (top) and recreational sport (the base). The wider/broader the base, the greater the chance that the teams at the top perform well. Sport clubs find it increasingly difficult to maintain the pyramidal structure in light of a levelling of performance and the decreasing size of the base of the pyramid. The sport managers of KDP tried to win back this base by 'buying' top performance outside of the club instead of choosing the top players from the base of KDP. From the members' point of view this strategy is wrong; yet the board's intention to develop a broader base (and therefore to restore the pyramid) can be seen as a strategy to sell the idea of a top level team to the members.

There are a few members who see agree with this choice and see the council's solution as innovative and of strategic importance for the club. Many other members however, think this choice does not fit the club. They have little motivation to get involved or to volunteer in the club. They suspect that sport managers are primarily furthering their own interests and show little concern and pay little attention to the membership as a whole. Sport managers reproach club members for lack of involvement with the club citing examples such as low attendance at general meetings and a lack of volunteerism. This lack of involvement by the membership means that sport managers focus more on the council itself than on the membership. Sport managers also have colleagues at other clubs and sponsors as their sounding board who react positively to their plans. The gap between the ways club members and the membership assign meaning can be described as an 'estrangement.' (Anthonissen, 1997). This alienation results in an undemocratic manner of making decisions, and an increasingly hierarchical and inequitable structure in an organizational form based on democracy, a horizontal structure and equity. This means that the club culture is in a state of flux.

The desire for integration

(Club) culture pertains not only to visible characteristics such as symbols and codes for behaviour but also to underlying assumptions or key values (Schein, 1985; Verweel, chapter 1 in this book). These are shared, often subconsciously, by many members of groups or clubs. If members share underlying assumptions then a certain type of integration occurs. Athletes do not become members of a certain club because they like the club colors or the way the bar has been decorated. Such outward characteristics may sometimes have a strong symbolic value but only matter when underlying assumptions are challenged. Elsewhere in this book Boessenkool (chapter 5) shows how this challenge of underlying assumptions influences mergers.

KDP sport managers who want to strengthen integration or unity in the club cannot resist emphasizing that a key assumption of the club is that 'top level teams should be embedded in a broad foundation'. They try to stimulate the feeling of belonging among members ('one big family') by emphasizing this underlying assumption or value. This means they pay little attention to sub-groups, subcultures and/or individual differences although many subcultures play a role in KDP: high level competitive teams, recreational teams, youth teams, girls' teams, indoor football, young people who do not want to play on Saturday, etc. In addition, sport managers who talk about 'we / they', openly show their preference for a specific group or team and/or focus only on the interests of that group when making decisions. The different groups and individuals try (if not always actively) to continually propagate their definition of reality and influence the desired unified culture.

The idea that consensus, unity and harmony are necessary in an organization, stems from an integration perspective on culture (Martin, 1992; Verweel, chapter 1 of this book; Verweel & de Ruijter, chapter 2 of this book) and from a systems approach to thinking about organizations (Mastenbroek, 1996). A similar perspective dominates public administration and organizational studies and in the empirical day to day practice (Verweel, 1995). In KDP the discourse about the pyramid is embedded in an integration perspective and is used to legitimate actions that (supposedly) promote unity within the club. Sport managers protect the pyramidal discourse through formalization and standardization although there are differences in meaning; if the club does not become unified by itself then that unity will be forced upon them. An emphasis on consensus and harmony is used to safeguard the idea of the pyramid. According to the club council, members who are not always concerned about unity or harmony challenge the basic assumption that a pyramid provides the best structure. The broader societal context plays a small part in the conscious decision making process of the sport managers. When they look outside of the club, they only do so to recruit new youth members (to broaden the base) to compare themselves to competing clubs, to look/search for sponsors and to strengthen the pyramid. In addition, they try to resist pressure from the town council and the KNVB. Of course the meanings assigned to sport in society play a role in the trend towards professionalization and in the creation of the pyramidal idea as a way to organize sport. We will return to this theme in the last chapter of this book.

The club's council allowed itself to be guided in its actions by several specific developments in the immediate context such as the building of a new housing development and perceived pressure from the KNVB. Giddens (1979) calls this 'event causality'. Sport managers see themselves as victims of top down structures 'that is how the system is; you cannot escape from it.' The council of KDP think it has no choice but to raise the level of play of the top teams and to develop a higher level of professionalization (see also Slack & Hinings, 1992). These two factors comprise the most important reasons for starting a foundation and a business club.

The influence of a market economy on sport clubs themselves is increasing. Many national sport associations encourage 'professionalization', such as is happening at KDP, for reasons of economics and quality. Participating in top level competition in amateur sport is seen as crucial in attracting sponsors. This assumption guides the actions of sport managers: 'We now are talking about a partnership: not only for the club itself but also for the individual members. Besides developing a KDP arrangement with discounts on credit cards and mortgages, we are thinking about savings programs for members.' The KDP council understands that a large(r) club is attractive to sponsors; the more members a club has, the greater the number of potential customers for the sponsors. It seems as if there is only one way of doing 'business.' The market -driven economy strengthens the pyramidal discourse, with its emphasis on top level competitive sport grounded in a broad base, in competitive sport.

United we stand; divided we fall.

The basic assumption that underlies the thinking about a pyramidal structure, can best be understood in terms of 'ideology.' The ways in which club members and the sport managers react and interact suggest that the idea of a 'pyramid' is a hegemonic discourse situated in an ideology in which top performance is assumed to take place under equitable conditions. An ideology gives the club the opportunity to create a seemingly unified front and is a 'temporary' but stubborn coagulation of constructions about which there is a great deal of consensus. Ideology refers to 'shared relative coherently interrelated sets of emotionally charged beliefs, values and norms that bind some people together and help them to make sense of their worlds' (Trice & Beyer, 1993, p. 33). Convictions are at the center of ideologies and directly and indirectly related to the interests that (groups of) people have (Verweel, 1987). What people perceive as social reality is directly related to the sharing of power: not just at societal level or within organizations, but also within the daily life of individuals themselves. The ideological is therefore 'the capability of dominant groups or classes to make their own sectional interests appear to others as universal ones' (Giddens, 1979, p. 6). This is what sport managers have been trying to do at KDP.

The KDP case makes clear that the sport managers perceive that top level performance means that the 'outside' world will notice KDP. The various relationships the council has in the world outside the club seem to justify to the KDP sport managers the path they have chosen. This 'justification' lessens their frustrations about the (lack of) involvement of members. Furthermore the large amount of money involved ensures that the feelings of responsibility and status of KDP sport managers increase. Some sport managers define this as serving their own interests; others see it as serving the (collective) interest of the club 'if we hadn't done this, the club would have gone downhill . . . this effort has prevented us from having to raise membership fees.' The council reasons that this plan has benefitted the continuity of the club which is important to all members. Accomplishments in the first division on Saturday KNVB can only broaden the base of the pyramid which in turn will ensure continuity of the club and the top teams. The manner in which the sport managers and club members handle this assumption and react to each other, points to the leaky nature of the hegemony of the pyramidal discourse.

Hegemony occurs when there is consensus about an ideology, making it the dominant ideology: 'The non-dominant groups and individuals concede spontaneously to the authority of the dominant group(s)' (Gramsci, 1975 cited in van den Brink, 1978, p. 16). The KDP case is a good illustration of how this works. Club members say they understand the need for top accomplishments in relationship to the pyramid. As long they have access to resources that enable them to play at their level, they agree with the 'pyramid' assumption as the sense making principle within the club. The chair, who has been with the club a long time, asks the small number of members present at the general meeting to 'trust' the direction the council wants to go. The members agree without one dissenting vote while in the hallways before the meeting there was much resistance to the idea. On the one hand, the members concede to the council's plans by voting for them; on the other hand, most of the members do not attend the meeting and/or are silent. They do so because nothing has changed for them ('recreation soccer has been paying the bill for a long time already') and because the principle of being part of the decision making process vanished a long time ago ('let them arrange everything . . . if they go too far, I am gone.') These members think it is good that the council is so involved and keeps the club going. The main concern of these members is not to be held responsible for the continuity of the club.

The pronouncements and behaviour of the sport managers and club members sustain and reinforce the hegemony of the pyramidal discourse. Hargreaves and Tomlinson (1992, p. 211) write that 'hegemony is not simply a question of ideological domination but also of processes by which social agents actively and consciously accommodate each other in pursuit of their perceived interests . . . ' Giddens (1979, p. 6) argues that, besides the role active and conscious behavior plays, interactions among actors are also influenced by passive behavior and can add to a defense of one's interests. KDP members and sport managers therefore influence each other by consciously not taking any action. People produce meaning within the context of interactions within relationships (Verweel, chapter 1 in this book).

Another aspect that sustains the hegemonic discourse in the KDP is the importance assigned to social cohesion. The potential of sport to strengthen societal cohesion is often cited by national sport organizations: 'Sport is the glue of society' (Kearny, 1992). A reference to cohesion was also made by KDP. At this (local) level the cohesive potential of sport is suggested and (re)produced in references to images of unity. As a result, disagreements and differences in meaning are discounted since they may negatively reflect on the interests of the dominant group(s). Still, it seems that references to cohesion are more counter-productive than productive for KDP. Since members are only encouraged to share the meanings given to the situation by the sport managers, the meanings that members may assign to the situation are not recognized. As van den Brink (1978) argues: 'that which is introduced at the ideological level does not reflect reality but the imagined nature of the relationships among individuals and groups' (p. 87). Meanings that members have, are welcome as long as they concur or reinforce the meanings of the sport managers. Sport managers accept that the individual or group experiences may not be totally congruent with the pyramid idea but are 'satisfied' as long as there is some agreement so that consensus can occur 'spontaneously.' Club members think the same way. As long as they see enough opportunities to participate in sport at their own level, then they will accept the reasoning of the sport managers. Yet if members sense that their own manner of defining the situation no longer counts, then they will leave and join another club.

Acceptance of differences in meanings

Inequality in power and differences in sense making result in council, groups and individuals within the club having different interests and concerns. Still the council seems to assume equality in power in the organizational structure of competitive sport and in the democratic decision making structure of the club. Possibly the way sense is made of (competitive) sport plays a role here. In competitive sport, the rules are the same for everyone. At the start of the competition everyone is seemingly equal. This is not true at the end of the event since then there are winners and losers. 'Our orientation is part of a system that gives everyone equal chances; equality is not the goal but a manner of attaining inequality' (van Baal, 1974, p. 45). Possibly this assumption made about competitive sport provides the framework for the manner of making decisions within the club. A (paid) membership is assumed to guarantee that each person has equal opportunity to participate in decision making at general membership meetings. Yet the situation within the club is marked by inequality since many decisions are made informally by a small group and formally put on the agenda at the membership meeting. This creates an oligarchy [5] (Michels, 1959; Horch, 1994; Ibsen, 1997). Members and council differ in and do not communicate the meanings they assign to their membership, their sport participation and their volunteerism for the club. This creates estrangement between council and members: experiences are not shared, meanings are not exchanged and, as a result, no new meanings are created.

The differences in the assignment of meaning in KDP (and many other sport clubs faced with a similar situation) are not used to create a starting point for creating meanings in an innovative way. The sport managers experience their difficulties as situations that increase uncertainty. This uncertainty results in an even stronger cry for unity. As Martin (1992) argues, the stronger the experiences of differentiation and fragmentation, the stronger the call to do everything possible to enhance integration. Most sport managers recognize that there is a diversity in sense making within the club but subsequently they reject the different meanings because their goal is unity and consensus. The blame for the high level of 'uncertainty' is placed at the feet of club members who engage in consumerism, who are spending less and less time volunteering for activities, and who suggest 'wrong' solutions (that is, they do not fit the perspective of the sport managers). There seems to be only one thing left for the sport managers to do and that is to use their power to safeguard the seemingly objective norm of top performance and to justify this by using the pyramidal discourse.

Self defined achievement: Room for diversity

Although the policy statements of national Dutch sport organizations assign importance to BOTH top competitive sport and to recreation sport, at the local level the members of the councils of sport clubs think and act using an image in which the foundation of the pyramid serves the top. Elements of both self defined and pyramid-related achievement can occur in competitive sport however. Crum (1991) defines competitive sport as a situation where an athlete simultaneously experiences the tension of a match, relaxes, engages in social interaction and defines 'success' for him or her self. We see that self defined achievement loses its meaning/significance in the development of club policies because the views of sport managers are limited to the objective norm of achievement which is tied to top sport (absolute achievement, status and income'). They believe that large numbers of youth must be taught to perform well. Sport managers of every club think that their club will become a second school for Ajax football players and that this is the only way to safeguard the continuity of the club. Although a few sport managers challenge this hegemonic discourse, most sport managers use this pyramidal image to guide their decision making. They find support for this way of assigning meaning by their colleagues which means that they are not quick to disagree with each other.

Anthonissen (1997) has shown that members of councils of sport clubs in other team and individual sports that are less popular (and therefore have less 'market' value) have the tendency to imitate clubs that do well in top-level competition and to use that as their legitimation. This imitation is one reason clubs increasingly resemble each other. A second source for this resemblance or homogeneity can be found in the (external) pressure from other organizations such as the local government and the national soccer association to 'professionalize' the sport club. Sport managers feel that they are dependent on these organizations. This dependency was reason for the KDP club to create a foundation for high performance soccer.

Ibsen (1997) argues that the way in which coaches are trained and educated also contributes to the homogeneity or similarity of sport clubs. Knoppers & Bouman (1996; 1998) have shown that the way coaches are selected and evaluated has a gender subtext: the physical abilities and capacities of males are the norm. This norm is seen as a 'pyramid related norm' and supports the focus on top performance and implicitly, the pyramid discourse. In addition, ethnic minorities are under-represented in club councils in the entire amateur Dutch sport world (NOC*NSF, 1998). In other words, most sport managers are white males. To what extent are the pyramid related norms tied to individual characteristics of male sport managers? How much room is there for those who think differently due to their social position?

Possibly, by taking differences seriously and exploring them, sport managers can develop new ways of making sense of sport and sport organizations. Some of them do question the pyramidal discourse and encourage decisions and policies that take the individual (athlete) as a starting point (Anthonissen & Boessenkool, 1998). A sport manager worries that 'young soccer players are taught that only winning counts; only first place counts. I am worried because for some sport managers that striving for first place has gone too far.' Athletes are also more critical and more inclined to stand up for themselves. KDP members, for example, left when their ways of assigning meaning where not heard or recognized. Consequently, sport managers must create more room for individual meanings and interests of different groups/members within the club. The power inequality in decision making between council and club members and differences in assigning meanings suggest that club councils must pay attention not only to processes of differentiation but also of fragmentation. De Ruijter (1996) argues that the diversity in (sport) organizations requires acceptance of differences and a coordinated vision in council policies and actions (see also Verweel and de Ruijter, chapter 2 in this book).

Sport managers need to pay more attention to individual, group and organizational issues. They must recognize and explore the extent to which individual histories, personal characteristics and differences in interests play a role in assigning meaning. Ideally then, attention will be paid to the meanings the sixth team, the group of older athletes, the women's teams, the youth who only want to play on Saturday, the Turkish team, and others assign to their sport participation and club membership. Sport managers should also try to recognize how gender, race, physical mobility, sexual preference and age may influence the sense making of participation and club membership. Allowing for diversity includes doing justice to self defined achievement in competitive sport. Management of diversity asks club councils to question the discourse about the pyramidal structure as the only possible discourse for amateur clubs in competitive sport. It requires the development of a new ideology (discourse) that will provide a basis structure (practice) for a club. This ideology has to assign equal value to different ways of defining performance and achievement.

Jan Boessenkool

Mergers: The political character of sense making in sport clubs

*'Someone who gives away the name and history of the club, doesn't care about the club at all'
(Member).*

'If you do not accept our proposals and decisions, then we resign' (Sport manager).

Overview

Mergers are an often discussed subject in sport clubs. There were about thirty mergers involving Dutch football clubs before 1990. Since then there have been about a hundred; in addition there are many ongoing talks about possible mergers. Several explanations have been advanced for this such as bigger is better is glamour (van der Stee, 1996), external pressure from sport associations and local governments, more regulations and fewer financial resources, and, the idea that small clubs cannot survive. Processes including that of mergers can best be perceived and analyzed from an arena perspective in which actors continually negotiate sense making. The political nature of these processes is very evident in merger processes. In this chapter I describe and analyze the assignment of meanings during the merger process involving two football clubs. I show how the dynamics of this process are in part unique to football clubs and simultaneously connected to contextual developments. The findings are based on research in which the mergers of involving more than 25 amateur football clubs in the Netherlands were investigated (Anthonissen & Boessenkool, 1998).[6]

The merger of Donaro and Bunder

Bunder, one of the oldest clubs in the Netherlands, was begun in 1908 as a secular club. Its top men's team has always played at a high level and much of the involvement of the club's members is in service of this team. Relatively little attention is paid to those who play at the lower levels and to the youth

75

teams. During the past several years, the number of (youth) members has been decreasing and the shortage of coaches and officials has become acute. Also, the making ends meet is a growing concern especially because the club's council wants to see its best men's team play at the top level which requires an expensive coach. In addition, sponsors who invest a lot in the club want results and a say in decisions about the club. In other words, the future of Bunder looks problematic.

Donaro was started in 1951 as part of the Roman Catholic movement toward emancipation. The membership list is filled with people with the same name because it is a family club. Although the top men's team plays at the lowest level of the KNVB, the club has always made ends meet. The former chair of the council says: 'If we needed money, we held a flea market that was always a success.' A pleasant and cozy social climate is valued more than top performance. The top men's team likes to win but the club is not prepared to pay exorbitant amounts for a coach. The number of (youth) members who play football is decreasing although the number involved in hockey is increasing. The latter may be because Donaro is situated in a relative wealthy village. A member explains: 'It is of course a village with standing; football does not have a high priority with us.' There is rarely a shortage of coaches and volunteers although it is these individuals who are having second thoughts about the merger. They fear that Donaro will be swallowed up by and disappear into the larger Bunder club.

There is no pressing need for the two clubs to merge but the sport managers of both clubs have noticed the merger mania elsewhere. The minutes of 12 December 1990 of one of the clubs reads: 'Close cooperation between the two clubs resulting in a merger, is the only way to keep football at an acceptable level; this is also necessary to keep the youth.' Such comments set the tone and the exploration period begins. The first talks accomplish little. The successive attempts are usually couched in discussions concerning finances and with sport itself. The discussions are unsuccessful for other reasons such as disagreement on a new name, the rehashing of old feelings and discussions dating to 1972, and, the seemingly unsurmountable differences in mentality usually attributed to specific persons ('we won't talk with him anymore'). When the assumption of equality between the two clubs is called into question, the independence of the clubs is emphasized 'We are a healthy club and can stand on our own feet' says a former sport manager of Donaro.

The village square becomes a place where all these matters are discussed since everyone in the village knows each other. The local media urge the village council to decrease its financial support of the clubs if they refuse to merge. A sport journalist writes ' . . . a merger of the two clubs has financial and organizational advantages and guarantees a more efficient use of facilities.' (local paper, 09-10-1992). The local government puts the clubs under pressure to merge by threatening with privatization and by implying that funds will be more readily available if the merger goes through.

Distrust and power struggles

Although little is accomplished in the following years, discussions to actualize the merger are begun in 1995. Differences in opinion about various matters are recognized but the emphasis is on financial matters. The merger will end up saving money. There are other, secondary, arguments cited in favor of the merger. A large club is assumed to draw more youth, result in a higher level of performance, attract more and better qualified coaches, lower membership fees, strengthen feelings of loyalty toward the club, increase the income from sponsors, permit the building of an indoor training facility and spectator stands, and, result in more clout in negotiations with the local government. The sport managers of both clubs expect that there will be several hassles about name and club colors of the new club but emphasize that all decisions should/will be based on rational and businesslike arguments and not on emotional grounds (minutes, meeting, 17-01-1995).

The process leading toward the merger can best be characterized by distrust and power struggles despite good intentions and positive attitudes. The chair of the merger committee is not associated with either of the two clubs and is well respected in the village. He recognized the possible pitfalls immediately already. At the first meeting of the committee, he proclaims that 'the fans, members and people outside the clubs will try to drive a wedge between the two clubs. We can only reach the finish line by using persuasion and forming a block.'

The distrust and power struggles are initially confined to the council meetings themselves with the chairs as key participants. They fight at almost every meeting about issues such as errors in the minutes, communication with the media, the club members and the representatives of the sponsors, the uniforms, and the bylaws. Rational arguments are usually used to end the discussion but the hatchet is never actually buried. Other sport managers sometimes choose sides or keep their distance. The chair of Donaro resigns after a half year. He ascribes his resignation to the delaying tactics of the Bunder chair who, according to him, keeps revisiting the duly recorded decisions. He accuses the Bunder chair of barely working for the merger and of leaking confidential memos to the press. Later he says his resignation has nothing to do with personalities but with the actions of the Bunder chair. Despite the resignation and 'personality' differences, the clubs continue on the path toward the merger while the battles continue to rage. To stop now means failure.

Most of the power in the clubs lies with the sport managers. The power inequality between sport managers and club members is so large that there is barely a struggle. The extent of the inequality in power between the two clubs is less clear and also, less accepted. Different situations such as geography (where one lives), religion (as a determining factor for club membership), structure (one sport or many) and the emphasis placed on top level competition determine positions of power. The chair of Donaro (a club that has Roman Catholic roots) for example, continually stresses equality and maintaining club identity while Bunder (high-level performance orientation) emphasizes the sport advantages in the merger. These differences in sense making continually underlie the discussions about integration, unity and consensus during the negotiations but they are not really recognized and accepted as part of the historical (and logical) differences. They are not allowed to make a difference.

These differences feed the underlying mistrust and the assumption of hidden agendas. Consequently, the negotiations are based on winning/losing instead of on a mutually beneficial situation. This zero sum win/loss situation often manifests itself in the nominations for sport managers for the new club. Will a chair be someone not affiliated with either club? Will every position such as treasurer, chair and secretary be shared? The latter option may be a short term solution but in the end it favors one club more than the other. The actual winners and losers are evident several years later.

Struggles on every front

The choice of the new club's name reveals the distrust and power struggle that have characterized the negotiations/talks. Club members are invited to submit ideas about and wishes for a new name in writing. The council decides that the recommendation of a commission, appointed for this purpose, will be binding. The choice of the new name, Synergus, is made by an external committee of three consisting of the mayor, a well-known ex-football player, and an advertising expert. Up to this point, club members have left most of the negotiations up to the councils but now are upset when confronted with the results. A sport manager sighs: 'You should never involve members in decisions about the details of a merger. They can have a voice and give ideas but they should not expect that their opinions will be honored.' Another sport manager thinks that it is better for the sport managers to decide the new name and club colors before the merger and then 'announce the decision to the members.' At the annual membership meeting of Bunder, 68 of the 69 present vote against the new name. The Donaro council warns its membership that they will resign if the name is not accepted. Letters to the editor appear in the local newspaper. One writer complains that 'the choice for Synergus reveals a total lack of fantasy. I argue for a real Dutch name.'

The mistrust is also revealed in the refusal (and inability) of the two clubs to share financial documents. This refusal/inability continues to erode the assumption of equal partnership with which the process was begun and continues even when the merger is formally completed. How large are the contributions of the sponsors? What is the value of the buildings and of the mortgage? etc. Both clubs have a sponsor and one of the chairs works for the sponsor. Who will be the chief sponsor now? In what manner will the sense making of the sponsors influence the merger?

There are other unforeseen complications. Discussions with city sport managers lead to more confusion because it is not clear what is agreed upon. One assumption, based on discussions with a city sport manager, was that the new club would receive a substantial subsidy from the local government. This turns out not to be true. Also, a sponsor wants (and gets) a seat on the council of the new club while the others do not want him there. The legal aspects cloud the merger even more. It is not clear what is required, what the difference is between a legal and practical merger, what the bylaws and club rules should contain, what the role of the KNVB should be, and, where advice about these matters can be obtained. In other words, there is much confusion and distrust. The merger, however, is unavoidable as it is seen increasingly as the solution to many problems, including finances and performance (of the top men's team).

Cultural differences between the clubs and emotional aspects such as loss of identity have moved to the background.

The merger is complete

After the merger is complete, the chair of Bunder says that the merger was about emotions and that nothing was gained it. He regrets the merger, 'not because of the members but because it was an organizational disaster involving sport managers, the KNVB and the village government.' His rival, the chair of Donaro, agrees and also cites the power struggle: 'Bunder dominated everything after the merger.' Many trained volunteers have left the club. Several of them say 'we do not come anymore because we do not feel at home.' There are few gains and many losses. The number of memberships of Synergus is less than half of what the combined two clubs had before the merger. Those who left have stopped playing or went to another club. Instead of moving to a higher level as was hoped for, the top men's team dropped to a lower level. In summary, the merger did not have the expected results.

We conclude that the creation of Synergus was accompanied by struggles on many fronts. Struggle results in victims. The daily struggle for dominance in the assignment of meaning is a struggle for power. The success of the sport managers is defined by the success of the top men's team which is synonymous with a successful club. It is primarily the sport managers who control the struggle in the merger arena.

The sport club as an arena: The construction of meaning

Unequal struggles

Before the merger, Donaro and Bunder were independent social systems each with its own historically determined structure and symbols. Slowly but surely its actors, especially sport managers, see their club as having to be in step with societal developments. The shortage of volunteers, complex rules and regulations, and finances are reason enough to act. The (lack of) performance of the top men's team also plays a role, especially for Bunder. Consequently the clubs leave a relatively peaceful arena and enter the turbulent arena of mergers. In this arena struggles take place that are related to struggles within each club and to between-club differences. Each confrontation brings to light the meanings assigned to a (hidden) part of the previous system and which sport managers had not previously considered. The struggle is continually about sense making: Whose meanings will dominate and result in action? Although Synergus is unique as a club, the process of its creation involves several patterns that are common to merger processes.

The sense making of sport managers dominates the process. They control what happens not only in the merger to create Synergus but also in other sport clubs. They use a hegemonic discourse in which they describe the ideal club structure as a pyramid and the club itself as a unified whole (Anthonissen, chapter 4 in this book). They vary in the way in which they define this however. The merger is begun with an emphasis on rational objectives that gradually disappear into the background. Cultural differences, power and emotions are the cornerstones in the construction/creation of Synergus.

The topics of the struggles change regularly but the past, positions, perspectives, meanings, and vested interests of the most important actors and the nature of the relationships with other actors, barely change. These are continually reproduced and characterize the tiresome merger process (Coenen, 1989). A few of the actors fall by the way side. Most of the struggles usually occur out of sight of the club members. The latter learn about the struggles primarily through the press or in other ways. In other words, their ways of making sense of the situation are influenced by the press and other actors. Power is both relative and relational however. All members have power but some use it more than others. Club members for example, can exercise their power by leaving the club. Obviously however, the struggle between sport managers and club members is unequal. Sport managers usually determine the direction of the club. The members' meeting has relatively little power. Yet the struggle among sport managers is a power struggle. Continually changing coalitions and strong-minded individuals try to guide the process in the direction they want it to go.

The actors in the struggle have various weapons. Some enjoy the support of a large group, some have a strong personality, and others have considerable knowledge about the situation and/or mergers. Groups that seemed homogeneous turn out to be heterogeneous and fragmented. The sport managers base their actions on their interaction with club members and with actors outside the clubs (stakeholders) such as the village council, the media and the KNVB. Although the stakeholders have relative little influence, their influence is assigned different meanings by the actors. In the following sections we will discuss the role of two stakeholders, the local government and the media.

Influence of the context

Local government as stakeholder

As Verweel (chapter 1 in this book) has explained, processes of change take place within a multi-layered context. In more than the half of the merger processes studied, the local government was an important stakeholder (Anthonissen & Boessenkool, 1998). The local government often initiates the idea of a merger (through their sport and recreational services) by constructing a policy intended to reduce the number of football clubs. Money/funding is the main reason for this policy. When the budget needs to be reduced, sport related items are the first to be eliminated. [7] Grants are cut and the rent for the fields is increased. In addition, land developers are very interested in the land on which the sport club stands. All these are reason enough for discussions between local government and the sport managers. During those discussions, it is obvious that meanings differ. The local city council prefers to have a few large sport clubs with a variety of sports at the edge of town. Sport managers suspect that the city government increases the rent to force the club to work on a merger and that the city only sees the financial side and not the sport or social aspects.

The struggle between government officials and sport managers usually does not polarize the two parties. Instead, sport managers assign their own meanings to the discussions and situate them in their thinking about the future of the club. They construct themselves as the victims of external developments and pressure. Simultaneously they turn this pressure into an opportunity to develop a more commercial and professional club. This is the reason why many clubs initially cooperate with the local government and hold high expectations for this cooperative venture. This enthusiasm wanes when it becomes clear that the local government's primary aim is to cut the budget, not to increase subsidies. The extent of to which this happens is dependent on the sport involvement of the members of the local city council themselves.

The high expectations the sport managers have for the involvement of the local government are replaced by disappointment and an increasing sense that the local government is more an opponent than a partner. Powerlessness and anger then shape the relationship. Sport managers see that local governing councils say much but do little. The councils of several clubs realize this early in the process and try to milk the situation for all it is worth. For example, if the sport fields have become part of the plans for a new housing development, the sport club uses all sorts of legal procedures to delay these plans until the local council gives them concessions.

Media as stakeholder

The press also becomes an important stakeholder in various ways during a merger. In the case of Synergus when an attempt to merge failed, the press accuses the clubs of wanting to hold on to their uniqueness and the status quo. The press feels that the uniqueness of the clubs is outdated and that it is time for local government to interfere by forcing the clubs to merge because a merger has financial and organizational advantages. The media argue that it is not correct to use city grants for each club if the clubs can function more efficiently and cheaper by merging. Such press coverage works to the advantage of sport managers who favor the merger. It encourages them to say they want to let go of the past and to make a new start based on an assumption of equality between the two clubs and using a business like approach. They see differences between the two clubs but describe them as differences concerning 'mentality' which should not play a prominent role in the process.

Similar discussions and struggles occur in the sense making process with the other stakeholders. Obviously then, the meanings created by stake holders can greatly influence the assignment of meanings within the sport clubs and can sometimes play a decisive role. Still, pressure from stakeholders does not create a united front. Much work must be done within the club to get the members to support the changes.

Layers in the arena

As Verweel and de Ruijter (chapter 2 of this book) point out, sport organizations, just like other organizations, are half-open systems with flexible boundaries. Processes within the organization are directly related to those outside it. Not only the context but also the arena is layered consisting of a front stage, back stage and under the stage (Bailey, 1977; Verweel & de Ruijter, chapter 2 in this book). The general members' meeting (front stage) used to be the most important and powerful place in the sport organization for taking decisions. Most of the members knew enough about the club to make informed decisions. Outside influences on club life were rare. Sport managers spent less time on decision making than on tasks such as keeping their eyes on the money; organizing party evenings, preparing for members' meetings, organizing teams, etc. This has changed. The front stage no longer shapes decisions but only takes decisions. The decision making process occurs among sport managers; this partially takes place formally in council and committee meetings (also front stage) but much is pushed to back stage and under the stage and is no longer visible.

Merger committees operate back stage. Their membership (and that of other ad hoc committees) is determined in an informal way by sport managers. In other words, the members' meeting has little say. Sometimes these committees receive a mandate from the members' meeting to explore merger possibilities but usually contacts have already been made with possible merger partners. The (local) football world is small and many people know each other. The nature of these contacts determines to a large degree the success of the merger talks. If sport managers, especially chairs of councils, can get along well with each other than the merger can be completed in several months. They work back stage and especially under the stage to be able to present their plan front stage (the general meeting). The members, who have barely noticed that these discussions were taking place, can only say yes or no.

In cases where the merger talks do not go well (back stage and under the stage), as was the case with Synergus, the chairs seek support among their members in various ways including at general membership meetings and through interviews with the media. Although it is the members who ultimately decides (at the general meeting), they do not have much choice. The fights for seats in the council occur back and under the stage. The members of the merger committee are well versed in the necessary information while other sport managers are happy if they are kept up to date. Decision making about mergers take place primarily within the councils of the clubs and even there the course of the merger is often decided by several people. A sport manager says: 'To ensure that a merger occurs, you have to get four or five people, who trust each other and work together based on strength not power, and then you will get the rest of the sport managers behind you.'

The sport managers rarely consult club members and often work independently of, or around their opinions and ideas. General membership meetings are poorly attended unless the merger is discussed. This increase in attendance in conjunction with a merger is perhaps because members are afraid of being taken over by another club, of losing their position on a team or as volunteer, and/or of losing club identity and climate. Sport managers then have to convince the membership that rationally speaking, a merger is the only way to go and that they, as council, will do everything possible to hold on to that that is unique to the club. In this way sport managers use the front stage to legitimate their back stage and under the stage behavior.

The power of identity and symbols

Most people want to be part of something and at the same time differentiate themselves from others (Verweel & de Ruijter, chapter 2 of this book). Music, drama, politics and sport clubs serve to meet the need for identification and social ties. Emotional and cultural ties become more pronounced during the negotiation process involving mergers. The strength of these ties can block or even stop the mergers. This resistance reveals the symbolic power of membership that rises above the financial and rational reasons that started the merger process. Although the meanings that members have assigned to their club membership have become more heterogeneous in the past decade, members do not want to give up the familiar during a merger. This is evidenced by the high attendance at membership meetings when mergers are discussed and especially when the name of the new club is on the agenda.

The struggle for a new name reveals the social value assigned to club membership. Most sport managers tend to attach relatively little importance the topics of name, date of incorporation and club colors or prefer to keep them at a distance. They are topics that can stop the merger process and in fact, some mergers have ended because the members did not want or like the proposed changes. Experienced sport managers suggest that the name should be settled first in the merger proceedings. Changing a name is an emotional experience because to most members it means letting go off the past or that the past is not important. A member says: 'Giving up the name is like dying a little; someone who just trades away the name and date of incorporation, does not care about the club.' The name is a symbol for all the members but more for some than others, especially for those who have been members for twenty to thirty years.

Some members argue that a totally new name should be selected because a combination name is always an expression of inequality 'You have to forget the differences and continue as one (club). ' This reflects a wish to start anew as a whole and to create a new culture. Members of both clubs however, often want a name in which they can recognize the old club. A combination name allows for this and keeps the past alive. Members see a merger as a necessary evil to survive instead of as a challenge for the future. Some see combination names as a reflection of a take over. The first named is the dominant party and takes over the second named club. This is true; after a period of time many members of the second named club have left because they do not recognize their original club in the merger club. They do not identify with the new club. They lose their tie with it and search for something else where they will feel like they 'belong'.

In general, the cultural and identity value of a membership in a sport club is miscalculated in mergers. Club membership obviously means more than having training facilities, having sponsors for shirts, and playing at a high level (the top men's team). The greater value of membership emerges because sport managers emphasize objectivity and instrumentality. Sport clubs are cultural practices that require a businesslike and professional approach according to many sport managers (see also Anthonissen, chapter 4 in this book). This perception is realistic but the question is if this reflects the (diverse) perceptions of the athletes themselves. Sport managers tend to underestimate the cultural-emotional meanings assigned to club membership. Of course, they themselves experience these 'losses' as well but their perception at the beginning of the merger process is different. At that time they see themselves as trying to keep the pyramid system intact (Anthonissen, chapter 4 in this book). If they strengthen the pyramid then their status as sport managers will also be higher. They begin to realize that their interests are only partially rational when it looks like they will lose in the power struggle. Subsequently they use such topics as the choosing of a name and the incorporation date to mobilize their supporters. In this way the members are important actors. A merger or a more businesslike approach may be necessary for survival but sport clubs are also cultural phenomena. Being a member means more than throwing or kicking a ball.

Sport managers as actors

The desire of sport managers to operate a sport club in a more efficient and business like manner does not stand alone but reflects societal trends. By emphasizing unity (pyramid) sport managers try to achieve their objective of having the best men's team participate (and win!!) in top level ocmpetition . It is the council's answer to the question of increasing diversity. Even the merger process (two or more clubs) begins with the assumption of diversity. Sport managers dream of large and healthy clubs in which the best men's team competes (and wins) at the top level. They discuss this with each other and with colleagues and slowly the fire of enthusiasm for fielding a top level team is kindled. Most members are unaware of this dynamic because they are more occupied with such 'mundane' aspects as the weekly matches, practices and being together. They will only sit up and taken notice if these 'mundane' aspects are affected. By that time the merger process is underway already. The struggle to strengthen the dominant discourse becomes more intense since that discourse will decide much of the nature of the future club.

The differences in 'mentality' that the press and most sport managers discount, play a prominent role at moments in the process when they give other meanings to 'merger.' Then financial and sport advantages do not seem so great anymore; they sometimes even assume that each the club can stand on its 'own two feet.' The actual negotiations involve various struggles and each sport manager strives to emerge as winner. This means that the various meanings gradually become congruent with the personal interests and objectives of individual sport managers. These are not necessarily in opposition to those of the council or club as a whole but they do ensure a struggle will occur. The assignment of meaning and the struggle for the construction of the dominant discourse is never smooth especially when there are multiple meanings involved in the struggle. Yet eventually the dominant discourse about finances and top performance wins and becomes the public discourse. Consequently the merger is the result of a power struggle, a forced unity without consensus or harmony. The alternate discourses have 'lost' but are not gone.

As we showed earlier, sport managers primarily use economically inspired reasons to decide to merge. They seek legitimization for it and for the meanings they give to 'merger.' Verweel & David (1995) point out the difference between economical and anthropological (personal) approaches to organizational processes. The economical approach focuses primarily on the physical, rational and business side of the club; the anthropological approach looks at what ties the club and sport managers to the club and affects them emotionally. The members agree with the economical approach until it affects them personally. Everything is all right until it affects their practices, competitions, bridge evenings, parties, etc. This is true of sport managers as well but they look at it differently. They want a unified club to ensure that the top men's team can compete at the highest possible level in KNVB competition; this in turn can give the club more allure and attract more members. This is also anthropologically based but the realization of this plan requires economic changes.

Sport managers present the economical approach on front stage but often fail to facilitate the merger process. Some perceive that the merger may mean a loss of identity but see it as a sentimental loss and do not realize and accept differences in sense making. The resistance is often not clear cut and unorganized. Those who resist usually do not have much power either. Only during and at the end of the merger process do sport managers realize that non-economically inspired perspectives and dimensions influence the processes and outcomes of the merger struggle and the arena as a whole.

Competition: Win and loss in the arena

Verweel (1987) argues that interactions in organizational processes are competitive. 'The type of weapons chosen, the cleverness of the parties involved, the prescribed rules and the positions that people take in the arena, result in inequality in power among the participating parties . . . The arena is not a playground in which the play assumes equality in the beginning and that the game can be started anew each time with the same resources, but it is sometimes a (merciless) competition in which earlier interactions have already been taken into account in position, status and even sometimes the structure of the struggle.' (p. 98). Sport managers conduct this struggle on several fronts: with club members, with the potential merger partner and with stakeholders. Positions (of power) differ and everyone has various (differing) weapons and skills. This does not mean that losers and winners are clear cut. The struggle can take unexpected turns due to the availability of new resources and the forming of new coalitions. The process has several 'rules' that are open to various interpretations. The strongest have the advantage but they are never completely in charge. Results are sometimes (totally) unpredictable.

Despite these characteristics of inequality, sport managers use the idea of equality frequently in sense making during the merger process. They suggest that there is equality in the beginning and in the results. Research suggests that this is rarely the case. Most mergers, including those in businesses, can best be described afterwards as a 'take over' (see for example Schenk, 1996; Verweel & David, 1995). The struggle is longest and more intense where positions of power are about equal. In the case of Synergus, there were no clear winners, only losers.

Characteristics of interactions in the club arena

The assigning of meaning is political. Negotiation and struggle about the hegemonic discourse make the sport club into an arena. Meanings exist, are contested and/or reinforced in the context of interactions (Verweel, chapter 2 in this book). This does not occur in predictable patterns since the contexts are complex and dynamic. Ideas do not exist by themselves but are assigned meanings by the actors involved, under differing circumstances. Most daily interactions occur in the same patterns that ensure that current relations and structural characteristics are reproduced (Giddens, 1979; 1984). This is more complex in mergers. Fear and uncertainty and dreams about the future characterize the sense making of sport managers. The predictability is less certain while the space for change is even greater. The merger arena is more turbulent than the regular club process. The ways in which sense making occurs become more explicitly visible. The results of this research suggest that the dominant perspective, situational specificity, multi-dimensionality, interdependencies, multi-layers, limited predictability, outcome orientation and competition/struggle are characteristics that change in intensity and form and determine how meanings are assigned in interactions and in sport clubs.

Conclusions

If we recognize that organizational processes in sport clubs, including mergers, are foremost struggles for (dominant) meaning then we can analyze these in terms of arenas over time. The characteristics mentioned in the last paragraph can be used to chart the processes by which meanings are assigned and struggled over. The use of the arena model as an instrument for analysis need not be just confined to the studying of merger processes but can be used for all organizational processes as long as we realize that they all have their own dynamics and context and a political nature. In this case study we focused on volunteer sport managers and club members of amateur football clubs in the Netherlands who were looking for answers in the society in which they live and participate. The acknowledgement of situational -specificity is the first step towards guiding the direction and shape of the sport club now and in the future.

Paul Verweel and Anton Anthonissen

Color blinds: Constructing ethnic identity in sport organizations

'A look, a tone, a movement of the body can be hurtful.' (Astrid Roemer cited in van Hoek & van Veen, 1997, p.9)

Overview

Faja Lobi fails to reach the end of the match

The game White Orange -Faja Lobi in the second division of the region Utrecht totally got out of hand yesterday. The referee Diks ended the match nine minutes before the end with the score 2-1, after a huge fight broke out among the players of Faja Lobi and the home team. Adri van Dalem of White Orange is crystal clear about who caused the violence: Faja Lobi. Errol Groeneveld, coach of the team from Utrecht places the blame for the violence in on the referee Diks and the goalie for White Orange, Arne Peypers. Van Dalem: 'our goalie made a brilliant save in the cross after which he was roughed up. Those crooks are quick to use their fists. A Faja Lobi fan chased one of our players with a knife 30 cm. long. Luckily the chair of our club was able to prevent the incident from escalating.' Van Dalem added that he would send an angry letter to the KNVB [Royal Dutch Football Association]. Groeneveld from Faja Lobi felt that the referee had failed to do his job. 'According to me, the referee left home with the idea of making it difficult for Faja Lobi. I continually told the boys to calm down which worked until number 4 of White Orange, pushed Geronimo Edwards. The goalie left the goal to come to his brother's defense. He began to hit and kick my player. ' Groeneveld did not consider it a tough contest. 'Football is our sport. We will probably get the blame. No, I am far beyond the discrimination phase. Every week we compete against 13 people. If it continues like this, we should consider withdrawing from the competition.' According to Klarenbeek, chair of the officials' committee, neither the referee nor his supervisor saw anything. 'Yes, we are not so happy with that. The referee felt threatened and advised that the police be called. This will be a difficult case for the Discipline Committee. I do not see Faja Lobi as a club of trouble makers.'

(Utrecht Nieuwsblad, 27 November 1995)

We take the time to let the newspaper article sink in; it is an account of a fight. As scholars and as athletes, we have seen and heard this before. Something was probably said, someone was kicked or someone was punched and beaten without the referee seeing it and it gets out of hand. Then we read that Faja Lobi talks about mitigating circumstances. We recognize the denial of the seriousness of the situation and the shifting of blame to the victims or the referee. Sport managers will never admit that their team or club was in the wrong. We have experienced the same thing ourselves. But then we see the name of Errol Groeneveld. We know him and know that he is an honest person. If he says that the official was at fault then we cannot blame Faja Lobi. Suddenly various meanings (frames) such as our own football experiences, our disbelief in the denials made by the fighters from Faja Lobi, and, our knowledge of Errol, collide. We now doubt the connection we made between the incident and the frame we used to interpret it.

Weick (1995) argues that the assignment of meaning always begins with three elements: an incident or experience (cue), a system of meaning (frame) and a connection (Verweel, chapter 1 in this book). Many connections are made in the Faja Lobi incident. To what extent does ethnicity play a role because a team with 'immigrant' players is involved? [8] Did the witnesses see a knife because they expected one when they saw 'immigrants'? New meanings produce new interpretations and more questions. Possibly the referee was wrong or this was an incident of discrimination. This discrepancy in assignment of meanings to the incident puzzled us as researchers and as athletes. We asked Faja Lobi if we could conduct a research study to explore the extent to which the created image of a highly volatile club with fans with knives is congruent with the culture of Faja Lobi. As Weick (1995) might say: Is the manner in which the cues get their meaning in a frame typical for the behavior and for the dominant processes of assigning meaning within the club Faja Lobi? After receiving approval from the club's sport managers we conducted interviews, observed the club in action, and, followed the matches of the top men's team for a year (Verweel & David, 1995).

Different frames

In our first reaction to the newspaper article we used several frames of meanings to describe the incident. If we examine the incident more closely, we see that it involves systems of sport specific, political and societal meanings at the individual, structural and social levels.

The 'immigrant' club as frame

Faja Lobi is an 'immigrant' club (Surinam) as compared to 'nonimmigrant' clubs that consist primarily of white Dutch players. Both 'immigrant' and 'non-immigrant' are 'fuzzy' concepts that function as abstract frames to create a place for the actual clubs themselves (Weick, 1995). The 'fuzzy' concepts mask a diversity of national and ethnic differences among athletes. Even the similarities within the various groups consist of abstractions. Members of an 'immigrant' club consisting primarily of people from Morocco, Turkey, Surinam and/or the Dutch Antilles have as little in common with each other as do members of a 'nonimmigrant' factory club, a Christian club or a village club.

Six percent of the Dutch population is described as 'immigrant' (Lagendijk & van der Gugten, 1996). Most (93%) who participate in sport are either member of a nonimmigrant club or train or play on their own. Only 7% are members of an 'immigrant' sport club. [9] The existence of 'immigrant' sport clubs is often perceived in a negative way. Most (95%) of the respondents in a survey conducted in Rotterdam are against the establishment of 'immigrant' sport clubs. The respondents favor such clubs only if they are temporary (Duyvendak, 1998). When the responses of 'immigrants' are examined, then 17% of them prefer to be members of an 'immigrant' club while 30% prefer a 'mixed' club. The remainder did not indicate a preference. Obviously the majority of the 'nonimmigrant' and 'immigrant' population prefers sport clubs to be 'nonimmigrant' or mixed.

Why then do Faja Lobi members want their 'own' club? A member says: 'You are seen as someone from Surinam, not as Dutch. And then it is very frustrating to describe yourself as Dutch. Often you are forced to face these facts, which is difficult. I am ambivalent about this. I feel more 'Surinam' than Dutch.' Another says: 'You begin to talk about 'us' and 'they' and behave that way. The danger in stuff like this is that you begin to confirm things that really do not exist.' Another says: 'The negative treatment of black players by the spectators has been going on for a long time. Clubs haven't done anything about this for years so they shouldn't be so hypocritical. For years they have created and allowed this [anti-black] culture to develop.' Swank (1996) who collected these quotations, concludes that discrimination within and outside sport creates feelings and emotions that are reason enough for 'immigrant' athletes to set up their own clubs so that they can participate in sport in their 'own' circle. [10] In other words, Turkish, Moroccan, Surinam and Antillean athletes often start their own club because of their negative experiences. This motivation is often judged negatively by 'nonimmigrants' who feel that separate clubs are undesirable (Janssens, 1998; Elling & de Knop, 1999). Experiences (cues) clash in the sense making in sport (sport frames). Meanings that evolve out sense making of sporting practices in which skin color leads to categorization clash with the dominant sport discourse that the only categorization in sport should be based on performance. In other words, the construction of meaning at the personal level clashes with the ideas about how sport should be organized.

The political frame

Politicians and social scientists have described Dutch society as segmented. For a long time various societal groups organized themselves in separate 'societies' (such as Roman Catholic, Protestant and secular) in which each 'society' had their own system of education, sport clubs, churches, and ideology. Each 'society' was represented at the national level. In other words, Dutch society was organized (and categorized) based on religious and societal ideology. Gradually these 'societies' have shrunk or are disappearing although they have not yet lost their influence (Goffman, 1961). The negative attitudes that 'nonimmigrants' have toward the establishment of separate sport clubs ignore this history. In addition, the Dutch constitution gives everyone the right to freely organize; in other words it permits organizations based on 'difference.' Setting up a 'separate' sports club is therefore a right and historically, a common social practice.

When large groups of 'immigrants' came to the Netherlands in the early seventies, the policies in the areas of welfare, education and in sport were based on 'categorization.' Each 'group' received 'different' attention on the assumption that their countries of origin differed as well. There was little concern for differences within such ethnic groups. Twenty years later that policy has shifted. The attention to difference has been replaced with an emphasis on 'ethnic integration.' This means that although 'immigrant' clubs are legal, they are politically undesirable (Lagendijk & van der Gugten, 1996; Janssens, 1998). 'Nonimmigrant' people have concluded that separate clubs do not enhance ethnic integration.

Sport policies concerning ' ethnic integration' usually define that to mean that 'immigrants' participate in 'nonimmigrant' clubs so that they have the opportunity to interact and mix with 'nonimmigrants' (Burgers et al., 1998). Success is subsequently measured by the degree to which the 'immigrants' assimilate the Dutch way of practicing, competing and organizing sport in general and the club in particular (Duyvendak, 1999). An assimilated male or female 'immigrant' competing for a 'nonimmigrant' club, adds to the performance level of the club, plays using the 'Dutch way', does volunteer work and speaks Dutch well. Government officials and sport members hope and assume that ethnic integration in sport also enhances or facilitates the ethnic integration of 'immigrants' in other segments of society. They hope and assume that sport participation can save 'immigrants' from being societal dropouts and reduce the crime rate.

The societal frames

The question of ethnic integration is not just confined to sport but is part of a larger question about societal participation of 'immigrants' in all levels of Dutch society. The most important societal marker of ethnic integration in the Netherlands is having a job. Entry into the labor market requires learning the language, the forms for social interaction, the expectations of Dutch society, and, the possession of certain skills and experiences. Education and schooling are seen as prerequisites for obtaining and keeping a job. The current debate centers on the way cultural differences among 'immigrants" themselves and between 'immigrants' and 'nonimmigrants' should be approached. Should 'immigrants' try to assimilate as much as possible? Do they have the right to segregate which permits them to be different or do they have a right to a multicultural society in which differences are accepted outside their own circles and seen as adding value to society? While politicians and sport managers emphasize ethnic integration in the form of assimilation (Entzinger, 1998), scholars point to the value of multi-culturalism in which differences are coordinated (de Ruijter, 1995; Roosevelt, 1993; Verweel & de Ruijter, chapter 2 in this book).

Three frames are commonly used to examine the participation of 'immigrants' in the labor market: deficiency, differentiation and discrimination (Verweel, 1998).

- The deficiency model is most popular and assumes that 'immigrants' are deficient in skills needed in the Dutch labor market. Consequently they are taught these skills (including lessons in the Dutch language) so that they can be 'equal' to the 'nonimmigrants.'

- The differentiation model assumes that both 'nonimmigrants' and 'immigrants' have to learn to handle the social- cultural and interpersonal meanings assigned to cultural differences. Managers and employees have to learn to accept and use each other's differences.

- The discrimination model searches for visible and hidden mechanisms in interpersonal actions and policies in organizations that serve as obstacles for 'immigrants'. These barriers are identified and removed through social processes and changes in regulations and inter-institutional relationships.

We see very little of these debates in the sport world (Elling & de Knop, 1999). The deficiency model, which is popular in debates about 'work', is rarely used with respect to sport skills. [11] Possibly this is because (male) 'immigrants', especially those from Surinam, are assumed to be highly skilled in sport. This stereotyping of the sporting abilities of male 'immigrants' not only pertains to top stars such as Gullit, Kluivert or Davis but also for the players of the seventh amateur level of Faja Lobi. The quality of their play is not controversial. In fact, often 'nonimmigrant' clubs recruit 'immigrants' to help them play at a higher level. The deficiency frame then works in a positive manner for 'immigrants' while 'nonimmigrant' players may perceive 'immigrant' players as a threat.

The lack of use of the deficiency frame, however, applies only to the athletes themselves. The deficiency frame is often used in sport to point to the short comings of 'immigrants', especially those from Turkish and Moroccan descent, in leadership and organizational abilities. Specifically, 'immigrants' are seen as 'deficient' in matters such as the timely payment of membership fees, the guidance of younger players by older members, and the compliance with all the regulations of organizational life. Ironically, many 'nonimmigrant' sport clubs have these same problems. These deficiencies pertain to 'nonimmigrant' clubs as well.

The differentiation model, which means learning to accept and work with differences, is used only with respect to sport participation itself. Differences in playing style, especially that used by players from the Dutch Antilles, Surinam and the Moluccas, are not only accepted but these players are often stereotyped as very skilled. Players from Moroccan or Turkish descent are stereotypically described as being quick and having a great sense of pride. Off the field however, the differences must be negligible, in other words' 'immigrants'' must assimilate in 'club life' (Elling & de Knop, 1996).

The discrimination model is used quite a bit in the sport world. 'Immigrant' athletes feel that they are discriminated against by 'nonimmigrant' club members, the referee and the opponents. Faja Lobi assumes that there are referees who have a difficult time accepting the nature of the club. There are referees who do not want to hear any Surinam spoken, who threaten the team at the beginning of the match with stopping it if there are problems, who give advantages to the other team, etc. (Verweel & David, 1995). We discovered in the first half year of our research that individual experiences and incidents affected the perspectives of the top team at Faja Lobi even when they had excellent referees. Such experiences are based on seemingly insignificant behaviors as the quotation at the beginning of this chapter suggests.

'Immigrant' athletes often place their experiences in sport in the context of their experiences of discrimination in the labor market and organizations, in the media, in racist humor and in ethnocentric films such as Tarzan. The stereotypes that parents of 'nonimmigrant' athletes hold about 'immigrant' clubs, as consisting primarily of volatile athletes, drug users and criminals, in part determines the nature of the interactions in sport. Many members of Faja Lobi see a connection between discrimination (frame) and many personal experiences (cues) ranging from the seemingly insignificant to highly charged emotional experiences. A Faja Lobi member describes walking into a 'nonimmigrant' club: ' When you come inside, everyone suddenly sits and there is no place left to sit. People go sit in an empty corner.' Members of the Faja Lobi club remember an emotional match: 'At a certain moment in a youth match, the referee of a match was very difficult. The coach decided to pull his team off the field because he could not guarantee their safety any longer. A parent of the opposing team scolded the coach using the term 'cancerous blacks.' The coach sprayed them with water from the water bottle. Six men beat him up. It is not the club but those parents.' (Swank, 1996, p. 18).

There are also problems within 'immigrant' clubs. A member says ' That really had nothing to do with discrimination but more with the temperament of those people' (Swank, 1996, p. 128). This quotation illustrates the importance of the frame in giving meaning to the incident (cue). Discrimination is a frame used by 'immigrant' and 'nonimmigrant' athletes and sport managers. The discrimination and deficiency frames, (the latter used in a positive manner for male athletes and in a negative way when describing leadership abilities) are used most often in sport.

The sport frame

Sport in general and football clubs in specific, are half-open systems (Verweel & de Ruijter, chapter 2 in this book). The economic, political and general societal context definitely influences sport participation and club life but does so within a specific situation. This situation is dominated by internal dynamics of relationships and frames in sport and the club itself (Anthonissen & Boessenkool, 1998). We explored this sport specific context and dynamics at an 'immigrant' club. We have argued earlier that the 'immigrant' club really does not exist. This fuzzy category is too diverse in daily practice to yield meaningful descriptions. Clubs labeled as Surinam, Antillean, Moluccan, Turkish and/or Moroccan differ too much from each other. We will therefore limit ourselves to the concrete situation of Faja Lobi. We will look at the sport specific and social and organizational situation of the club.

Faja Lobi

The referee whistles often making many choices during a match. We notice that Faja Lobi never reacts when the call goes against them. In one match, for example, a totally wrong flag signal of the boundary official of Faja Lobi is ignored. Neither team comments on this. When Faja Lobi is not given two possible penalty situations there is no reaction. A player of Faja Lobi is kicked hard by an opponent and lies hurt on the field. The opponents throw the ball back to Faja Lobi because of the way the injury is handled. Faja Lobi plays against an opponent with whom there had been problems previously. The opponents need to win this match if they wish to advance to a higher division. Before the match, an opponent hands a bouquet of flowers to the captain of Faja Lobi to congratulate them on advancing to the higher division already. The match could have been volatile but it develops in a peaceful manner although the boundary official of Faja Lobi is ignored three times and a goal by Faja Lobi is disallowed for unclear reasons (Verweel & David, 1995). These examples suggest that many situations occur during a game that requires frames to generate meanings about them. The insider frames tend to be narrowly focused whereas 'detached' outsiders (like us as researchers) can see other possible frames.

Organizing the club

Surinam students began Faja Lobi in 1961. The club has a large social and sport function (Verweel & David, 1995). It is busy every day of the week, even when there are no sport events. The (small) restaurant/bar functions as a meeting place for various groups of men, women and youth, athletes and nonathletes alike. About 80 spectators attend home contests.

The members of Faja Lobi mirror the multiethnic nature of the Surinam population: Creoles, Hindus, Javanese, Indians and Chinese. Members also come from the Dutch Antilles. Morocco, Spain and Poland. A few Dutch 'nonimmigrants' are also members of the club. The multiethnic context of Surinam means that members want to have a multi-cultural club. Members learned about the club through their networks. Many young boys who have played for a 'nonimmigrant' club and either did not make the top team or did not like it there, have joined Faja Lobi. The few members who leave the club are the very talented boys and repatriates.

The club has sufficient volunteers to fill all the technical, organizational and administrative positions. Sport managers regularly visit the bar, are spectators at the matches and/or coach a team. Council meetings are held once every four weeks and can be stormy. ' Sometimes bad things happen in the council room . . . the things that are said!! But when we finish the meeting everything is OK again. We get along well with each other. You would never see two people in the bar with tension between them. We keep business and personal aspects separate.' Another member says 'We have a few hard working boys in the council but sometimes their communication with each other is lacking . . . This means that sometimes meetings are unnecessarily long' (Swank, 1996, p. 7). An agenda, to which points can be added, is used to conduct the meetings. Everyone gets a limited time to speak. The club is in good shape financially although it took a while to get there. The current sport managers have made agreements with those to whom they owe money and have agreed upon certain financial rules and regulations. The books are sound and healthy.

This description of Faja Lobi clearly shows that this is no 'problem' club. In a certain sense, Faja Lobi is like a typical Dutch club that values its social life highly. Faja Lobi has a social value for those who come from the same social category and is characterized by social ties that make it a hospitable club. The club is reasonably organized and plays good football. There are no indications of dangerous situations developing and potentially volatile situations are ignored.

Connections

Our research debunks the image of Faja Lobi as a dangerous club. As scholars, we see little evidence of discrimination. How then can the uproar surrounding the incident described at the beginning of this chapter be explained? The answer can be found in what Weick (1995) says: 'A cue in a frame is what makes sense, not a cue or a frame alone (p. 111). As scholars, we used neither the ethnic integration nor the discrimination frame to study the club. This meant that we assigned meanings to our observations that were different from those assigned by the participants in the incident.

The importance of frames is illustrated in the incident with which we began this chapter. It is easy to dismiss this as just an incident. The members can only remember three such similar events in the last ten years. Yet everyone knows about this incident and that discrimination played a central role. The opponents ('nonimmigrants') see the incident as confirming the image of Faja Lobi members as fighters. Some will be certain that they saw a knife. They are using a (different) frame for giving meaning to their experiences. This is quite different from the frames used by other 'immigrant' clubs to talk about Faja Lobi. Sometimes fights occur during those matches too but there is no talk about discrimination. Any match can result in a fight but always followed by a handshake; it has nothing to do with the club but only with fighters.

It is Faja Lobi's color that limits the 'nonimmigrant' athlete to using the ethnic integration frame for making judgments about the club. The existence of 'immigrant' clubs is judged negatively which means that similarities between 'immigrant' and 'nonimmigrant' players are not even seen. It is the same color that makes Faja Lobi members blind for any frame but the discrimination frame. It means that all the positive incidents are forgotten and that a wrong look or remark ('I still have to work tomorrow') can only be heard as discriminating.

Color blinds and does not discriminate

Politicians and government employees are also often blind; they find the old image of separate clubs (separate societies) undesirable because differences in sport should not be categorized and organized on the basis of difference. Faja Lobi is not connected with a specific societal cause. Moreover, the multi-cultural character of Faja Lobi cannot be compared in any way with the total character and demographic membership profile of 'nonimmigrant' clubs. The ethnic integration perspective most often used by policy makers does not reflect reality for 'nonimmigrant' clubs either because they are also organized along lines of social class, faith, gender, sexual preference, age and validity (Coakley, 1998). Similarly, 'immigrant' clubs have also become more heterogeneous.

Verweel & de Ruijter (chapter 2 in this book) describe integration, fragmentation and differentiation perspectives. Differentiation processes dominate sporting practices yet 'nonimmigrant' athletes and creators of policy (which includes 'immigrants' as well) want ethnic integration. Ethnic integration usually means that 'immigrants' adapt to the strategies, organization and social principles of the 'nonimmigrant' club. Fragmentation is a possibility only if we accept that 'immigrant' clubs develop similarly to 'nonimmigrant' clubs. A frame that fits the development of the sport clubs and players and that is powerful enough to be an alternative to the currently dominant frames of discrimination and ethnic integration is needed to manage sense making of such situations. This alternative is a sport specific variation of the societal and institutional frame: management of diversity.

The management of diversity frame starts with the desire for and possibility of the recognition and acceptance of differences between and within 'nonimmigrant' and 'immigrant' clubs. Differences can be used positively in social and sometimes, instrumental ways. The differentiation between and within sport clubs, sports and people is always an expression of fragmentation. Individuals and sport organizations need this fragmentation to develop their own identity/meaning in relationship to the other (including own ethnicity). In other words, we need the 'other' to be ourselves as persons, as athlete and as sport club. The identity of the other is important at every level: individual level (left wing versus right back; technical player versus speed demon; strong header versus passer); social level (hospitality versus competition, seniors versus youth, men versus women), and, institutional level (working class versus upper class, city versus rural, faith versus secular). Not the integration of these differences but the management and coordination of these differences on all levels are important in managing diversity.

The management of diversity frame is not just a theoretical construct or socially desirable construct. It is gaining more popularity in the economic sector due to reasons of profit and continuity. Businesses are beginning to feel the limits of the ethnic integration and discrimination frames because they no longer can neglect the multi-cultural potential in the work force and clients. They are forced to switch from an integration perspective to coordination (recognition, acceptance and use) of differences. These societal developments and sport specific practices can lead to sense making that creates new meanings using the 'other' as reference point. Many 'nonimmigrant' sport clubs have already found it necessary to accept difference in order to survive. To keep their members (continuity) they must do justice to the differences within the club. This applies to 'immigrant' clubs as well. The current color blindness can then be exchanged for the insights offered through the management of diversity frame and can mean that many experiences (cues) such as winks, remarks, fights and tackles receive other meanings.

Jan Boessenkool and Frank van Eekeren

The nature of sport and international cooperative development

'These exercises of the Dutch coaches are really great. But you know, I need 25 balls for these exercises and in the place we come from we only have one ball for 25 players. So what can I do? And what about these beautiful grounds and the equipment you've got in Holland? We have to share our grounds with the whole community and I can only use Coca Cola bottles as cones!!' (South African participant in the Dutch Coach the Coaches program)

Overview

Experts, including those from the Netherlands, travel with increasing frequency to Third World countries to work on sport projects. One such project is the Coach the Coaches program, a joint initiative from the Royal Dutch Football Association (KNVB) and the South African Football Association (SAFA). Both the organizers and participants are enthusiastic about this project yet things have gone awry in a way that can best be characterized as a misfit between donor and recipient. In this chapter we explore how it is possible that what seems so clear cut can go wrong. Why are policy makers and those who work in the area of international cooperative development (ICD) unable to match the needs and adapt to the situation of the recipients? We also explore the current meanings sport has for ICD and that ICD has for sport. We will examine these meanings using a cultural and sport specific perspective.

The case study that we describe here is based on the report of van Eekeren (1997) in which he explores the significance the project had for the various actors who were involved. The research was conducted over a period of six months in the Netherlands and in South Africa at the conclusion of the project. The results were obtained through qualitative methods such as participant observation and in depth interviews. The analysis of this case study is based on an exploration of the implications and consequences of the use of hegemonic concepts such as 'underdevelopment of sport in Third World countries' and 'two-sided nature of sport.' We end with suggestions for an alternate discourse.

Sport and international cooperative development (ICD)

Although the globalization of sport has a relatively long history, sport has just recently come to the attention of those who work in ICD. Sport used to be seen as an unnecessary luxury that was unimportant in ICD and in for some, sport was a vestige of colonial relations (Swank & van Eekeren, 1998). Most of the attention in ICD has traditionally gone to health, agriculture, infrastructure, structural development, good governance and the development of democratic processes. Sport, especially football, is however, part of daily lives of millions of people in those countries. The World Cup madness and hype were greater in countries such as South Africa, Morocco, Nigeria, Cameroon and Brazil than in the Netherlands. A KNVB instructor said, after visiting Zambia and South Africa, 'I learned what is important in Africa: ABSOLUTELY first is football, then eating and then sleeping and last of all, work. Football is inconceivably important there; unbelievable!' We can be astonished by this and/or we can accept it and see it as a new opportunity for ICD. This message has already been understood by the commercial version of ICD and slowly but surely other sectors of society are beginning to grasp the role sport plays in society. [12]

Individuals from all the corners in the world, including the Netherlands, assume that sport can play a significant role in individual development, in the improvement of health and well being, and in enhancing societal cohesion (Coakley, 1998). Yet when sport becomes part of ICD policies, other dimensions play a role. Those who work in ICD and in sport have the tendency to think and act according to 'outdated' ideas about culture, sport and differences. They see the sport situation in Third World countries as backward and underdeveloped and intend to help those countries to 'catch up'. This way of thinking reflects a 'traditional' relationship between donors and recipients.

In addition, the last decades have seen a growing interest in the possible meanings that sport may have for a society. Dutch policy makers in sport and to a lesser degree, government officials in ICD who know less about sport, tend to rely on functional perspectives about sport as exemplified in a concept called the 'two-sided nature of sport.' (see for example Steenbergen & Tamboer, 1998; Knoppers, chapter 8 in this book). Sport is seen as an instrument that can be used to achieve societal objectives such as personal development, integration, identification, health and well being, equity and personal satisfaction (Digel & Fornoff, 1989). Both sport managers and governmental officials tend to use this functionalist approach, perhaps because it so easily translates into measurable objectives and methods.

This two- sided- nature- of- sport perspective sees sport as having its own unique essence (intrinsic value) and simultaneously as being an instrument (extrinsic value) (Steenbergen & Tamboer, 1998). Steenbergen and Tamboer (1998) stress that the intrinsic and extrinsic aspects should be kept in balance. Those who use the 'two-sided nature of sport' approach attempt to define and place various aspects of sport into the extrinsic and intrinsic categories. This categorization has become the dominant Dutch discourse for looking at sport. Thinking in terms of sport intrinsic and extrinsic aspects is relatively clear cut and assigns specific and easily understood functions to sport. This is attractive to those who work with measurable objectives and functions. In this chapter we will explore the results of these ways of looking at sport and at ICD when they come together in projects in sport ICD such as in the Coach the Coaches project.

Case study: Coach the Coaches

The (sport) boycott against South Africa ended when apartheid formally ended. The necessity of helping South Africa develop sport at the top, at the township and at the rural levels has caught the attention of the international community. Most but not all the attention has gone to top sport. Those affected by apartheid have become a new target group for ICD. Western donors are especially active in the large and politically interesting townships such as Soweto and Alexandra. The goal of several projects is to keep the youth off the streets and to attain educational objectives. The KNVB and SAFA worked together on one such project, the Coach the Coaches project.

The Coach the Coaches project evolved out of another project called SCORE, which was sponsored by the Dutch government by way of the Dutch Olympic Committee (NOC*NSF). A representative of the NOC*NSF in South Africa heard that the SAFA is interested in working with the KNVB. The Dutch 'actors', that is, the KNVB, the Dutch embassy in Pretoria and the Department of Health, Welfare and Sport (VWS) are informed of this and seem to be interested/ willing to pursue it. Based on the results of a pilot study conducted in 1993, the Dutch actors decide that structural and institutional cooperation between the

KNVB and SAFA is desirable and that it fits in the program to help black South Africa 'catch up.'

The KNVB asks the NOC*NSF to make an inventory of the wishes of SAFA. The conclusion of this fact finding mission is that the SAFA wants Dutch assistance in setting up coaching education courses analogous to those in the Netherlands. The subsequent grant proposal, written by the KNVB, is accepted by the Department of VWS. This proposal is congruent with dominant Dutch perceptions about the functional nature of sport, that is, that societal objectives can be achieved by using sport as instrument (extrinsic nature of sport). The Dutch will provide the content and arrange the practical aspects of the project. SAFA however, is less enthusiastic than the KNVB suspects. The agreement primarily mirrors what the Dutch want. SAFA recognizes the high quality of the Dutch coaching education program but does not want a carbon copy. SAFA has other interests as well. It wants to work with the KNVB at the top sport level, that is, their primary objective is to host a match between the Dutch team 'Orange' and the South African team 'Bafana Bafana.' This wish however stays unexpressed for a long time.

Another culture, another situation

Since SAFA has no clear wishes concerning the coaching education program, the KNVB decides to offer regular courses ('clinics') in South Africa. The people from the KNVB who are involved in the project have little, if any, information about the context and situation in South Africa. In addition, no agreements or plans are made for subsequent steps beyond the holding of the clinics. The first clinics are held in 1996. The late date (three years after the idea is conceived) is due to problems in South Africa and, as the KNVB realizes later, to the fact that SAFA was not quite prepared for the project.

SAFA has delegated the responsibility for the organization of the project to a sponsor and a marketing firm who see commercial opportunities in the project. Suddenly there are more South African actors, each with their own interests, involved in the project. SAFA works 'front stage' but there are others with a great deal of influence involved 'back stage' (Verweel & de Ruijter, chapter 2 in this book). SAFA also has trouble discerning and differentiating among the various Dutch actors and their interests. The formal agreement is with the KNVB but the interest of and the financing by the Department of VWS and other actors play a role. Moreover, the interests of the KNVB are not clear cut either. The coaching course is given as it would be in the Netherlands, perhaps because of the international respect that the Dutch coaching education program has enjoyed in the past. In other words, the context of the project has several layers, is situationally specific and more complex than was first thought.

Starting the project

The Coach the Coaches project in South Africa is formally open to both whites and blacks, women and men, old and young(er). Yet blacks and coloreds between 20 and 40 years old form the majority of the 140 participants. There is only one female participant. Obviously the structure and design of the project do not automatically lead to a demographic balance. Little attention is paid to the demographics of the participants during the entire length of the project.

During the clinics, held in four different locations in South Africa, the KNVB staff and SAFA coaches meet each other for the first time. The South African coaches are surprised by the presence of the Dutch instructors. 'They sent two old men. We expected top coaches. They could have shown us more respect.' Moreover, the course seems to offer nothing new. 'There wasn't too much that I grasped there. I have had a lot of introductory courses before.' The needs and wishes of the target group, the coaches, had not been not considered in the planning of the project. A Dutch instructor observes: 'The final goal of the project was that the coaches would instruct others but who? The majority coach children in the townships but others were school teachers or coached in a club. These require different approaches.'

The circumstances and facilities are totally different than when the courses are given in the Netherlands. The Dutch methods cannot just be transplanted into the South African setting. The quotation with which we opened this chapter is a good illustration of this mismatch. South Africans live in other circumstances, in another culture, and possess qualities of which the Dutch are unaware. A South African coach explains: 'We had interesting discussions with these old men. One day they were explaining to us that passing the ball with the outside of the foot wasn't right because you cannot give straight passes. So I said to them: "Give me a ball and I show you how we do this in South Africa." So I gave a straight pass with the outside of my foot. They were amazed . . .; you know our technique is far better than the Dutch!'

Interpersonal communication is also complicated. A Dutch instructor attempts to make sense of his experiences and says: 'Our [teaching] method is based on a lot of talking, giving each other positive feedback. The South Africans were not used to this. They do not do that and respect authority. We also discovered that disagreeing with older people is not part of their culture.' Obviously the Dutch and South African organizations involved in this project do not have sufficient insight into the needs and wishes of the target group.

Various ways of making sense

The management and council of SAFA show little interest in the grassroots project, that is, the clinics. 'SAFA only believes in Bafana Bafana [national team]. They don't believe in development. They are not interested in our problems. That is why they do not support us with finances nor equipment, not even with words!' says a coach from Durban. A coach speaks for many when he says: 'SAFA needs the sponsor's money. And the sponsor uses us, the coaches and the KNVB, for their advertising campaign! They come only to impress the public.' In short, the suspicion is confirmed that only Dutch wishes and the interests of the South African sponsors play a role in the setting up and holding of the courses. Differences between and within organizations and a lack of clarity from SAFA contribute to this perception.

The project continues on its way. The KNVB comes to South Africa to discuss the continuation of the project with the sponsors and the marketing firm. When the KNVB people arrive in Johannesburg, they discover that the sponsor has already printed and distributed glossy brochures containing an overview of the program for the coming month and of the contribution of the KNVB. The KNVB knew nothing about this and SAFA is disappearing into the background. According to the brochures, the KNVB will educate several national coaches who subsequently will conduct courses at the grassroots level. SAFA invites 40 coaches to attend a continuation course in Johannesburg. Nine coaches will be selected from this group to attend a two-week course in Zeist, the Netherlands.

The interpersonal histories, concerns and emotions and, deeper issues continue to play an important role. The region north of Johannesburg, for example, is not represented in the continuation course. Several people say that this absence is due to a disagreement between a coach instructor and a SAFA sport manager. In addition, another coaching course, organized by another sponsor of SAFA, is being held simultaneously in the same complex and is labeled by the SAFA representative as 'the real SAFA course . . . They are the real coaches of South Africa.' Obviously there is a great struggle among commercial interests for the product 'football.'

This visit of the KNVB suggests that the arena of the Coach the Coaches project is larger, has more layers and is more complex than originally thought. Consequently it is no wonder that activities are not coordinated with each other. The competition among the 40 South African coaches for the nine tickets to the Netherlands increases. The mistrust is great. An instructor from the KNVB says: 'Those coaches were afraid that the people from SAFA would select other coaches behind closed doors.' Emotions and interpersonal relationships of the actors surface and shed new light on the context and on the processes of sense making.

The nine coach-instructors are finally selected and have the opportunity to take in all the dimensions of football in the Netherlands. The KNVB allows them to look behind the scenes as well. This results in some dissatisfaction among the visiting coaches as they realize that several things need to be changed at the organizational level in football in South Africa. A coach-instructor says: 'To realize that in South Africa there is no structure . . . that's sad! I am telling you: our national office cannot compare to one of your district offices. Our time in Holland made clear that we have to work hard . . . ' Neither the SAFA nor the sponsors welcome these types of comments about organizational structure. They feel that the coach instructors should confine their comments to football. They say: 'We are not in Holland, we are not the KNVB!!' This is further evidence that the Dutch program does not fit the South African context. The content of the project is assigned different meanings by the various South African actors. It is quite 'Dutch' and not adapted to the South African situation. A South African coach-instructor sighs: 'Sometimes we had to realize that we were in Holland to learn and share ideas, not to change.'

The KNVB expects that it has built up much credit with the SAFA after the four clinics, the continuation/selection course in Johannesburg and the two-week course in Zeist. Yet these efforts by the KNVB do not mean that the SAFA automatically prefers them. The SAFA chooses a German, for example, to be the director of coaches while the KNVB had expected to fill the position. The relationship between the KNVB and SAFA becomes guarded after this.

Yet the Dutch and South African men's teams do play a practice match in Johannesburg in June 1997. This match means that SAFA has realized one of its most important objectives. The KNVB admits that it understands little of the way SAFA operates. Cultural differences are cited as a possible reason for this. But is this the right answer? Or was there little desire to work together in the first place? Or did the SAFA have ways of sense making that the Dutch failed to recognize because they were different from their own? Did the Dutch base their reasoning on dominant ideas about culture and assumptions about the nature of sport?

Communication among actors

An important conclusion of the research into the Coach the Coaches project (van Eekeren, 1997) states that the Dutch who were involved (people from the KNVB, the Department of VWS, and the NOC*NSF) had the tendency to reason in an unidimensional and homogeneous way using their own context as starting point. The integration perspective (Martin, 1992; Verweel & de Ruijter, chapter 2 in this book) dominated their thinking. The context differs however not only for the different organizations involved in the project but also for the different staff members *within* the organizations.

The sense making of Dutch sport managers and government officials, not South African football players, is the central focus of the project. The feelings and personal involvement of Dutch sport managers and government officials have played a large role in this. Their own experiences and the dominant discourse in the Netherlands serve as their guidelines and become embedded in the project. Discussions about the project take place primarily within their own work circles and exclude the recipients. There has been little, if any, acknowledgement of interpersonal, cultural, historical, and situational differences. Ignorance of interpersonal and cross-cultural differences means that expectations are also unexpectedly diverse. As the beginning of the project approached and the contacts with the South African actors grew, the diversity in expectations became clearer and some adjustments were made, primarily through trial and error. Yet because the perceptions of the South African coaches remain subordinate to those of the Dutch, the results of the project are less than expected.

Why did the Dutch actors not use the information and knowledge gained through their interactions with South Africans? Is this a result of an uncritical acceptance of a functionalist perspective of sport as described earlier in this chapter? Is this due to the complexity of intercultural management that is dependent on interpersonal interactions and relationships and in which cultural differences, interests and emotions play a large role? Is every actor a prisoner of her or his own context? We will explore possible answers to these questions in the next paragraph, not to accuse those involved, but to gain insight into the processes, to raise awareness of the actors' roles and to search for 'playing room for change' within personal boundaries. This means that more room can be created for diversity in sense making and to incorporate the ideas of the recipients in the planning.

Putting the concept of 'culture' into perspective

The various actors involved in the Coach the Coaches project do not always understand each other. The discussions between the KNVB and SAFA, for example, do not always go as the Dutch expect. The immediate reaction, also often described in the organizational literature about cultural differences, is to blame the 'other culture' and to work within a framework of stereotypes about that culture (Peters & Waterman, 1982; Deal & Kennedy, 1982; Hofstede, 1992).

To what extent are cultural differences between the Netherlands and South Africa responsible for the decision of the KNVB to give its own courses in four South African cities? Or can the relationship between the SAFA and KNVB be characterized by the dependency of the 'smart' recipient on the donor who tries to 'sell' its own perspective on football? Do cultural differences between the KNVB and the Department of VWS result in a lack of clarity about the project or does the dependent nature of the relationship between the donors (VWS and KNVB) and recipients (SAFA and coaches) also play a role in determining the direction of the project? Do cultural differences between the headquarters and the regional offices of SAFA result in problems or do interpersonal rivalries and emotions play a larger role? The Coach the Coaching project clearly shows that all that is problematic cannot be attributed totally to cross-cultural differences. We explore possible answers to these questions by looking at the 'cultural diversity' approach.

First, South African culture is as heterogeneous as the culture within the Department of VWS. Secondly, the explanatory power of a cultural difference approach ignores two important aspects: the individual and the context. The interactions among individuals and members of organizations are not only influenced by cultural background but also, especially in this case, by relationships of power, by self interests and by personal emotions.

International development can be seen as a form of intercultural management (Vink & Schapink, 1994). The question after so many years of ICD is what is 'cultural' and intercultural'?. The Dutch like to describe ICD as 'searching for bridges, bridges across cultural gaps.' This idea suggests that the meanings assigned by the donor and the recipient are equally important. The analysis suggests however, that ICD more often than not, only reinforces the status quo. The one- best- way strategy still dominates ICD and is exemplified by the KNVB's decision to offer its successful Dutch coaching courses in South Africa. This ignores the specific situation in South Africa.

An alternate way of sense making

This one- best- way strategy fits in the integration perspective described by Martin (1992). Possibly sport managers and those in ICD assume that globalization has led to a standardization and uniformity within the world of football. This vision is often described as McDonaldizing (Hannerz, 1992). This perspective assumes a trend or movement toward cultural convergence or growing sameness and represents the classical vision of modernization seen as a steamroller that denies and eliminates cultural differences that get in its way (Verweel & de Ruijter, chapter 2 in this book). MacDonaldization represents simultaneously the theme of modernization and the theme of cultural imperialism.

Another perspective on globalization and ICD emphasizes differences (Verweel & de Ruijter, chapter 2 in this book). Advocates of this perspective emphasize the need to recognize cultural differences among various groups. They point to problems of alienation and displacement that occur when cultural differences are denied or suppressed (see also Anthonissen, chapter 6 in this book). 'Stamping out cultural variety has been a form of "disenchantment with the world"' (Nederveen Pieterse, 1996:1389). The notion of cultural difference is also often connected with identity politics and policies, with gender issues, with rights of minorities and indigenous peoples (see Knoppers, chapter 3 in this book). Differences are often seen as unproductive, as being short term and changeable, and primarily as generating rivalry and conflict. The KNVB seems to be using this differentiation perspective in their sense making. The problems that emerge during the project are attributed to the 'fact' that SAFA is different. The cultural differences are so great that they are seen to interfere with 'normal' working relationships.

As an alternative to the integration and the differentiation perspectives, we prefer a third position in which we see fragmentation as structural (Hannerz 1992; Latour 1994). Some call this process 'hybridization' (Verweel & de Ruijter, chapter 2 in this book). It emphasizes the idea that global powers are - and will always be - quite vulnerable to very small scale and local resistance. Hybridization acknowledges that 'communities as well as the people engaged in them, are always in flux, divided, contested; groups and individuals are perpetually escaping them as well mobilizing to enforce them.' (Kalb, 1997, p.240). This hybridization perspective is closely aligned with the fragmentation perspective (Verweel & de Ruijter, chapter 2 in this book).

Donors and recipients: Making sense of the relationship

Policy making by donors is sensitive to trends, especially those in its own country. The key points of ICD in the Netherlands keep changing. The recipient countries have grown accustomed to this and primarily try to survive. Their dependency on grants often pushes them to implement the policies of the donor countries. Representatives of target groups in ICD have become professional and smart/strategic recipients who know exactly what donors want to hear and see in a grant proposal. Consequently there is little room, if any, for local perspectives and values.

The actual activities of the project Coach the Coaches are not based on the wishes and needs of the target group. They are the result of interactions/ discussions among the various actors and the meanings they assign to the situations, to relationships and to ICD. The case study illustrates how existing relationships are reproduced in daily interactions. Clearly cultural and communication differences in themselves do not play a large role in daily practice but receive their meaning within the context of the relational aspects of ICD. That the Dutch send older coaches to South Africa is not a problem in itself. In fact, South Africans might appreciate being instructed by such respected men. The previous history of this project ensures that the presence of the old men taps into another reaction.

The cooperative effort has everything and nothing to do with cultural differences. Is there, for example, a difference in cooperative ventures inside the Netherlands and those involving South Africa and the Netherlands? Possibly social interactions, in which the result is determined by the meanings assigned by the actors during and after the discussions, play a much larger role. The assignment of meaning is of course, a socio- cultural process. Blommaert (1995) says 'I have never seen cultures communicating with each other, confronting each other or having a conflict with each other. I have however seen contacts and conflicts between individuals and institutions, each time within a specific historical, social, cultural, political and situational context but never as ideal carriers of an objectively defined culture.' (p.9). The analysis of inter - or intra-organizational interactions as processes of sense making therefore, requires a contextual approach.

The two-sided nature of sport

This case study yields several insights about sport and ICD. The Department of VWS underwrites this project because it included societal objectives such as individual development and well being. These may not be the goals of the coaches but seem to belong only to the Department of VWS. The organizations that carry out the project, such as the sponsors, KNVB and SAFA, agree to these objectives in principle but work on furthering their own interests. The printing of the glossy brochures by the sponsor gives the KNVB little playing room. The Dutch courses are used in the project with the assumption that their content would help the South African coaches reach the stated objectives.

These differing interests make it difficult to collide with ideas about the two-sided nature of sport. This approach fails to consider that the categorization into 'intrinsic' and 'extrinsic' is done by concrete actors in concrete contexts. A dialectical relationship always exists, that is, reality is always situationally defined. The meaning that the South African coaches assign to the Coach the Coaches project is totally different from that assigned by Dutch coaches to the same courses. Some South African coaches see the course as an ideal way to spend their time ('I want to live football every minute of my life!!') and as part of their personal development. Others view the course as part of a commitment to their community ('I had the opportunities that other people in my community didn't have.'). In addition, the meanings assigned to football in South Africa as

THE sport of blacks and colored are quite different from those given to it in the Netherlands.

Agreement on the assignment of meaning to sport may be impossible since the definition is always dependent on actor and context. The definitions of actors should minimally be equally valued and can change over time. Trying to establish a meaning of sport for everyone that will still count for tomorrow and the day after that, reflects a static and normative approach. Experience with the Coach the Coaches project has shown that flexibility in coping with ever changing circumstances is a key factor to 'success.' This flexibility is antithetical to a perspective that sees sport as having a dichotomous nature.

A focus on sport as instrument may also mean that most of the attention is given to achieving societal objectives based on the perceptions of the donor, the Dutch. The assignment of meanings by the recipients, the coaches in the townships, becomes secondary. The results of the project shows that giving instruction to coaches to enable children in the townships to play football in organized competition, does not ensure that this will stimulate the development of these children beyond their ability to play football or that cohesion within the township will increase. In other words, the meanings assigned to the project are dependent on meanings assigned to sport (and ICD) by the various organizations and actors involved with the project and the interaction processes among them. Sport cannot be viewed as separate from the actors and the context in which it takes place.

Dialogue between donor and recipient

We argue for an actor in context approach in which we pay attention to the dialectical nature between the actors and their contexts (Anthonissen & Boessenkool, 1998). Power, norms, definitions/meanings and emotions are the major resources that actors can draw upon in their doing/work. These resources are always used within a context, not a vacuum. The context is complex because it is layered, multidimensional and situationally specific (see also Boessenkool, chapter 5 in this book). This complexity is apparent in the Coach the Coaches project. The focal points are the interactions among individuals who are influenced by their context. Discussions between the head of education programs of the KNVB and the chair of the SAFA for example, occur in a multi-layered context because the time, place, previous discussions, latest developments in the general and job context, topic, interests, emotions, etc. decide the course of each discussion.

The general context of the donor's country, not the recipient, tends to be the most relevant determinant for determining the donor's course of action. Government (and football) officials tend to be more intent on pleasing their superiors/government than the recipient. Although the KNVB has honorable intentions in offering assistance to South Africa, it also needs a good working relationship with the Department of VWS because it is a major grant giver and it develops rules and regulations that affect football. The same can be said for the SAFA. It needs its sponsors more than it needs to have a strong relationship with Dutch organizations. We conclude that the agency of actors is of an interdependent nature, determined by the worlds they live and work in and in which decisions are based, in part, on strategies that compare the different needs and interests with each other.

Effecting change

The foregoing may make it seem that actors are prisoners of their context. This is true in a sense but not totally. The place, the nature of the walls and the design of the prison can be altered. Systems can change when relations among actors (structure) change (Giddens, 1979; 1984). Actor and structure are in a dialectical, not oppositional, relationship. This dialectical relationship gives actors room for implementing structural change. Current relationships may be deeply rooted but they are produced and reproduced by all those involved. Actors can exert influence on current relationships especially in a new policy area such as sport and ICD. Sport organizations and ICD organizations are new partners and therefore establish a 'new' relationship within the structure of ICD. New relationships can possibly be developed in interactions with each other and with partners on the other side of the world.

Effecting change also requires insight into the structure(s) and the context of the actors who are involved (Giddens, 1979; 1984). Historical relationships and traditions play a role of course. Relationships of dependency are difficult to change but insight into the 'arena' in which one is acting is crucial. This arena and context are constantly changing, as we said earlier. A raised consciousness is not just confined to an examination of the situation but is an ongoing process in which learning and doing are inextricably linked.

This way of seeing (fragmentation) has consequences for those who make and those who implement policy. A structuration perspective assumes that everyone who is involved with the writing and implementation of policy can act and that every action has meaning. The creation of room/space for the contribution of every actor requires openness. It means that objectives cannot be established ahead of time and that it is almost impossible to construct precise objectives and to know exactly how an ICD project should/will develop.

The formulation of policy therefore, requires flexibility with respect to expected results and the actual content and conduct of activities. Those who create policy need to keep in mind the reasons for the project without requiring concrete measurable results. Those who implement policies need to be very sensitive to the contributions of others and be very flexible in their work. Both groups need to give a project room to develop and take its course. This approach means that the usual methods used to evaluate ICD projects may not be suitable because they tend to fix the course and content of the project. The use of 'monitoring' during the project may be more suitable than the measuring of results at the end.

The use of instrumental /functional ideas about sport and ICD in current policy seems to create a situation in which the needs and wishes of the target group fade into the background. Those who take part in sport may not see it as an instrument for development. Many boys and girls may dream about becoming famous soccer players but they play primarily because they like it! As a South African coach said: 'You know to be honest, I don't care what you people in Holland think or do. I live here in this mess, but as long as I can play football it's all right!'

Annelies Knoppers

Managing diversity? Sense making in sport organizations

Overview

We began this book by looking at the process of sense making and the ways in which individuals use it to assign meanings to their experiences in society and sport organizations. We then looked at how a specific social position, in this case gender, may situate an individual with respect to processes of sense making. Four case studies dealing with professionalization, merger, diversity based on ethnicity, and international cooperative development explored the different but similar ways in which sport managers make sense of their experiences in (sport) organizations. In this closing chapter I explore the commonalities and disparities in the various case studies and try to place the chapters of this book in a broader perspective. I focus primarily on what a movement from the dominant integration perspective to the rarely used management of diversity might mean for sport managers.

I begin by exploring the predominant use of the integration perspective on organizational culture. How do sport managers deal with differentiation and fragmentation? How and why do they attempt to create consensus/unity? Most of the case studies show that sport managers wrestle with many issues and realize that change is needed. Yet they use primarily the integration frame to deal with differences they encounter in managing these issues while the authors in this book argue for a management of diversity approach. I explore the implications of using of this approach and argue that such an approach entails two things: 1) including and hearing voices representing a diversity of social positions and 2) using a critical perspective to look at sport. I discuss how sport managers tend to use a functionalist perspective to assign meanings to sport participation and an integration perspective to manage sport organizations and show how these perspectives are incongruent with the management of diversity approach. The possible congruency of two other perspectives on sport (conflict and critical) with the management of diversity perspective on organizations is then explored.

Differentiation, integration, fragmentation

Every author in this book has pointed out how diverse the meanings are which are assigned to the *organization of sport*. Although many actors described in these case studies recognize (some) differences in the assignment of meaning within their sport organization, they often interpret those differences negatively. In other words, although differentiation exists within sport clubs, sport managers and administrators prefer (and often assume) integration (consensus). Although they recognize differences, they do not want those differences to make a difference. The case studies about mergers, about professionalization (pyramid) and about ethnic integration (Faja Lobi) reveal that actors often recognize that differences exist but see them as undesirable if they get in the way of a unified sport club. Most sport managers define a unified club as one in which most of the members agree with the dominant discourse of the council or sport managers. In the case study about the attempts to professionalize a sport club, we see that council members do all they can to ensure that everyone sees that a pyramidal structure is the best and only way for the club to survive. These attempts to erase differences fits with Martin's (1992) point that the stronger the experiences of differentiation and fragmentation within an organization, the stronger the call to do everything possible to enhance integration.

As Verweel (chapter 1 in this book) shows, meanings are continually being (re)produced as actors try to make sense of the 'what, why and who' in their different 'worlds'. These worlds include their participation in sport, their tasks as sport managers, their role as sport fans, their home life, their responsibilities at home and in paid labor, in the community, etc. Sport managers also (re)produce specific meaning about sport. In several case studies, meanings are assigned to *sport* that define it in terms of top performance and being 'competitive.' In both the professionalization and the merger case studies the (possible) improvement of the top men's team is used to persuade others to agree with the plans of the sport managers for the future of the club. Similarly, SAFA wants coaching education courses but more importantly wants their national men's team to play the Dutch team. Sport managers and administrators tend to believe that top sport or performance builds social cohesion and fosters local, national and international pride. Top sport is assumed to work as a magnet and increase the number of sport participants at lower levels. The question is to what extent do sport managers and administrators who use the pyramid discourse identify primarily with top sport or with the base of the pyramid? I will return to this topic later.

As the different authors of this book point out, unity or consensus does not exist in sport organizations. Sport managers and officials who want integration where differentiation exists, have to work to establish *their* discourse as the dominant discourse. In other words, they try to build consensus for their discourse or coerce the members to accept it. Obviously there are different ways of obtaining consensus; the predominant one in use by sport managers in these case studies is by persuasion. In the story about sport and international cooperative development, South African coaches attend the clinics and courses because they love football and/or because there is a chance of 'winning' a trip to the Netherlands. In the merger and in the professionalization case studies, club members are promised a 'better' (more stable) club if they agree to the proposed changes. Similarly 'nonimmigrants' collectively use stereotypes to persuade themselves and each other that an 'immigrant' club is 'dangerous'.

Sport managers do not only encounter differentiation however. At some levels, sport managers do see/experience unity/consensus. Knoppers (chapter 3) points out that most of those holding leadership positions in (sport) organizations are unified in their acceptance of the dominant discourse that their organizations are gender neutral and that meritocracy prevails. This in itself is not surprising because most of them are white, heterosexual middle class males who tend to benefit most from this discourse. This unified stance on gender neutrality and meritocracy contrasts with the different meanings assigned to 'belonging' to a club by the athletes. The various case studies show how sport managers are supported in their ideas by other sport managers and stakeholders who support the dominant discourse, that is, they think the same way. Grant giving agencies, sponsors, the media, local and national government officials, and, administrators from national sport organizations take on stakeholders' roles. They also tend to represent the same social position as most of the sport managers. Sport managers see homogeneity when they are with colleagues and stakeholders. Most of the differences that sport managers encounter come from the ways athletes make sense of their participation in sport.

Another way of reinforcing a hegemonic discourse is to ignore alternate discourses or to use them selectively, an option primarily open to those with power. The history of women in sport, for example, shows that when women have developed alternate discourses about competition and performance, they tend to be ignored and marginalized. Similarly, the name Synergus is chosen as name for the new club (after the merger of Bunder and Donaro) although the members vote against the name. Many members of KDP do not want to see their club professionalized in such a way that means that much of its energies and resources flow toward the top men's team. Sport managers circumvent the concerns of these members by creating a foundation and a business club. Satisfying these sponsors (stakeholders who cannot be ignored!) is perceived to be more important than attending to the different meanings club members assign to their membership.

Those who seem to have the least voice in the decision making processes are the athletes themselves. This does not mean that they are passive victims however; they use their power in various ways: by distancing themselves from their clubs, by grumbling/ dissenting, by not attending general meetings, and, by leaving the club. Some athletes establish their own clubs like those at Faja Lobi did.

Management of diversity

In every case study in this book, the methods used to achieve integration 'fail' to a certain extent because the number of members at the clubs, excluding the 'immigrant' club, declines. Not surprisingly then, that a much repeated conclusion in this book is that sport managers and administrators need to accept fragmentation (ambiguity) and use a management of diversity approach. The management of diversity frame (see Verweel, chapter 1; Verweel & de Ruijter, chapter 2 in this book) begins with the willingness to recognize and accept differences (in the assigning of meaning to sport and the organizational nature of sport) between groups and individuals and within groups. Verweel and de Ruijter call this 'coordination', which is a recognition, acceptance and use of differences not with the purpose of integrating them but managing and coordinating them at all levels. This concept of diversity however pertains not only to meanings athletes assign to their sport participation but also to power inequities associated with social positions such as gender, race/ethnicity, sexual preference, etc. These receive very little attention in the stories in this book with the exception of the story of Faja Lobi.

As I indicated in the previous section, those who currently dominate leadership positions may be ill equipped to handle diversity of meanings (among members) because their colleagues hold similar social positions and are likely to articulate similar discourses. Sport managers may not be accustomed to 'hearing' and/or taking seriously alternate discourses that arise from those who are positioned differently as a social group. Few, if any managers, show concern about this lack of social diversity.

The case studies in this book are incomplete because they only present differing views within a particular social position. This in itself is not 'wrong' but the use of a unitary standpoint epistemology can be problematic when it is not acknowledged and when it is assumed to be the only possible framework or the perspective that counts for everyone. Most of the chapters in this book are rooted in a masculinist Eurocentric perspective. This is not uncommon. As Slack (1997) argues, accounts about organizations are usually men's accounts of organizational reality. The case studies describe primarily the experiences of male sport managers, athletes and administrators. The chapters describe the world of sport (organizations) as seen through the eyes of white men. This is not to say that all male sport managers think alike (we have seen enough examples of differences!) but the voices of women managers, administrators and athletes are often missing. This is not surprising given that social life, including that in (sport) organizations, is influenced by the 'relative power of men and women in society and by who does the theorizing about society' (Coakley, 1998, p. 31). The viewpoint of how women, as women, experience these different situations is absent in the case studies Yet their viewpoints(s) are essential because they may in part help to create that 'playing room' (see Boessenkool & van Eekeren, chapter 7) in which change can be rooted.

Other voices are missing as well. The voices of 'immigrants' are heard only in the case study about an 'immigrant' club (Verweel & Anthonissen, chapter 6). Yet the same chapter shows that most immigrants who are involved in sport are members of 'nonimmigrant' clubs. Where are the voices of 'immigrant' sport managers? Similar questions can be asked about the absence of sport managers who are positioned differently with respect to gender, race/ethnicity, sexual preference, age, and validity (disability). This lack of diversity of people represented in the case studies is reflected in the (lack of) alternate discourses among sport managers themselves. The discourses of other groups that are often marginalized in sport play a minor, role, if any, in establishing an alternate discourse. It would have been interesting for example, to hear the story about the football project in South Africa from several South African perspectives. Or perhaps a Surinamese could look at a 'nonimmigrant' Dutch club and observe the way the members and sport managers assign meaning to their participation and to the organization. When we talk about managing diversity therefore, we have to ask questions about who is doing the managing and who defines what 'diversity' is. Possibly then management of diversity also includes a commitment to ensure that those holding leadership positions represent a diversity of people themselves with respect to social position such as gender, sexual preference, age, race, ethnicity and (dis)ability.

To what extent is a movement toward management of diversity approach enough to bring about change in sport organizations? Are sport managers able to recognize and accept differences in the assigning of meanings to and within organizations? Are they able to accept and work with diversity in sport? There is an abundance of literature available on the management of diversity (see Verweel and de Ruijter, chapter 2) and on social homogeneity of managers (see Knoppers, chapter 3) yet very little of that knowledge has been applied and used in the Dutch sport world. Why do those holding leadership positions in sport consistently favor the integration perspective? To what extent is it congruent with their perspectives on sport? Possibly a management of diversity approach means that those working in sport need to let go of assumptions not just about organizations and social relations but also about sport. Research shows that most sport managers and administrators tend to use a functionalist perspective in looking at society and sport (Anthonissen & Boessenkool, 1998; Coakley, 1998). To what extent is this perspective congruent with a management of diversity perspective?

Functionalist perspective

A functionalist approach to sport assumes that society consists of systems held together by shared values and by consensus. This approach is held by people 'who have a vested interest in preserving order and stability in society' (Coakley, 1998, p.34). Functionalist assume that institutions personify everyone's collective interests and therefore, that everyone has an 'equal' share of power. Functionalists tend to assume that sport plays a positive role in society and in the lives of individuals; they tend to see sport as having various (positive) societal functions such as social integration and cohesion, as playing a role in nation building (top sport), in enhancing health and well being, in providing opportunities for the 'safe' release of tensions and frustration, and, in strengthening international relations. Sport is seen as a democratic institution because everyone participates under the same rules and often against people of similar abilities. In some sports, such as golf and horse racing, handicaps serve to equalize the competition even more. As Knoppers (chapter 3) points out, this assumption is one reason many sport managers assume that sport is gender (and race/ethnic) neutral. If women and ethnic minorities are not represented (proportionally) as coaches and sport managers than that lack of representation is attributed to their 'deficiencies' (see also Verweel & Anthonissen, chapter 6). At the beginning of this century sport was organized primarily for upper class men); now a century later it is assumed that everyone who wants to, can participate. There are enough 'rags to riches' stories of athletes to 'prove' this idea.

Managers and administrators who use a functional perspective to look at sport often assume that the most important and essential part of sport is its competitive aspect. In other words, the essence (or uniqueness) of sport is the striving for 'best' or 'top' performance. Ideally speaking, sport is assumed to build social cohesion; practically speaking, this may mean 'top sport. Top level play is assumed to have a trickle down effect, that is, it motivates others to become involved in sport or to join the 'winning' club. Sport and competition are defined as being synonymous, a definition that has become hegemonic (Coakley, 1998; Hall, 1996). This belief in the unchanging essence of sport can reinforce the assumption that sport managers have about the homogeneity and social cohesion of sport organizations. 'Although sport practices embody specific and identifiable purposes, values, and meanings, they are typically viewed by both participant and spectators as ahistorical and apolitical in nature . . . Moreover, sport leaders tend to view themselves as impartial facilitators operating in a value-free and ideologically neutral setting' (Sage, 1990, p.11/12). This (erroneous) belief in an unchanging essence is illustrated in the case study about sport and international development. It was assumed that South African coaches can be given the same coaching education courses as Dutch coaches not only because the program in itself is excellent but also implicitly because sport is sport, the world over; everyone plays by the same rules and use the same skills.

Sport managers are not the only ones who often view sport from a functionalist perspective. As Coakley (1998) points out, the functionalist discourse about sport is frequently used by the media, by scholars, by government officials at the local, national and international levels, by national and international sport officials (and their organizations), etc. Athletes may view sport in a functionalist way as well; it may be the reason they participate in sport. Possibly also they accept the dominant functional discourse because they have very little choice if they want to participate in organized sport. Most athletes are aware of who controls their sport clubs and their sport opportunities; occasionally they have protested (but rarely collectively).

Throughout the history of sport there are examples of individual athletes who have, fought against rules and opportunities that marginalize or exploit them. A Black boycott of the 1968 Olympic Games, for example failed; yet two Afro-American athletes did publicly protest against the way they were exploited. They gave the black power salute as they stood on the medal stand during the medal ceremony. They felt exploited because they were expected to win medals for the sake of their country while they were constantly marginalized because they were black. The reaction of sport officials to this salute is an example of the way power can be used by sport managers and administrators to reestablish hegemony. The athletes were stripped of their medals and banned from Olympic participation in the future.

Coakley (1998) has pointed out that athletes often invest too much physically and emotionally in sport to be able to protest collectively or to reflect on the possibilities of other choices and opportunities. They rarely have the opportunity within organized sport to assign their own meanings to sport and to have those meanings taken seriously by sport managers as several case studies illustrate. Too often they have learned to accept the situation and/or let themselves be defined by it. If change is to occur, athletes and managers need more choices and opportunities that challenge dominant ways of thinking about sport. Without those they may adopt the prevailing functionalist view on sport or drop out of sport.

By taking only a positivistic view of sport, functionalists tend to ignore the possibility that sport can continue to exist even when it is dysfunctional. Sport managers, for example, who assume that sport is a democratic institution may fail to see that sport benefits some (social) groups more than others. They may be unaware that government officials and managers of sport clubs, of the KNVB, and SAFA benefit more from their way of organizing and assigning meaning to sport than do the athletes and even the coaches. Sport managers may ignore the fact that a pyramidal structure usually privileges a men's team. The possibility of constructing several pyramids in a sport club (one for men, one for women and/or one for older and one for younger members for example) is not mentioned by the managers in any of the case studies.

Ironically enough, although the top of the pyramid is usually occupied by a men's team, functionalists tend to see sport as an instrument for ethnic/racial (social) integration. The question of clubs organized along lines of ethnicity (or on the basis of sexual preference or gender) is regarded by functionalist as undesirable and as fostering social inequality (Elling & Knop, 1999). They may overlook the possibility that 'nonimmigrant' clubs contribute more to social inequality by marginalizing certain social groups than that they serve the interests of a diversity of individuals. Faja Lobi is probably a better example of a multi-cultural club than most 'nonimmigrant' clubs are, probably because it began as a Surinam club and not as a white ethnic majority club. Its incorporation was rooted in marginalized ethnicities. The organizational nature of most 'nonimmigrant' white male dominated sport clubs and organizations may therefore promote the vested interests of those with power and therefore enhance social inequality.

Obviously then the confluence of their functionalist perspective on sport with their integration perspective on organizations, may make it difficult for sport managers to effect change in sport organizations. If those in the sport world believe for example, that social order requires consensus to function properly and that sport participation contributes to that consensus, then it may be difficult for them to abandon the integration approach. If sport managers believe that sport is an inspiration for society and that sport integrates ethnic minorities or can be used to build or enhance social cohesion, then they may find it difficult to blend that belief with a management of diversity approach because the latter requires another way of looking at society and at sport organizations. Yet as is evident in the case studies, sport managers do see that change is imperative so the need for change may perhaps push them to consider another way of making sense about sport.

Conflict or economic perspective

Some may argue that the actors described in this book use more than only functionalist approaches. At times sport managers also seem to use a conflict approach. The conflict approach sees sport as influenced by economic forces. There are many examples in this book where economic forces play a major role in shaping the decisions of sport managers. The KNVB and SAFA use grants (for the development of South African football coaches) to strengthen their own position in various ways: as the developer of coaching education courses (KNVB), to attract sponsors (SAFA), and at the same time, to satisfy grant givers (governmental agencies). Members of an 'immigrant' sport club use their experiences of being discriminated against in the work force to assume that they will be discriminated in sport. The sport managers in the merger and the professionalization case studies want to use current market forces to professionalize their clubs. They (re)produce a discourse that link a high level men's team to enhancing the participation of all athletes although ultimately it means that the top men's team receives the most attention (resources and publicity). As stated earlier, it is assumed that the better the team performs (entertainment), the more athletes will be attracted to the club and possibly join it. Most research however, suggests that sport as consumption, as a form of entertainment, does not necessarily encourage people to go out and participate or become involved themselves (see Coakley, 1998). Yet this economic argument is often used by sport managers.

The sport managers portrayed in this book who use market forces to attain their goals do not however, look critically at the economic forces. They show little awareness of the impact that market forces have on their decisions and the implementation of their ideas. There is little evidence that they are aware of the role these forces play in enhancing social inequality in their organizations. They use economics as a way of reinforcing their own positions (of privilege). In contrast, a sociologist or anthropologist who uses a conflict perspective is likely to point out how sport is organized to benefit many sport managers! It is highly unlikely that many sport managers therefore, would use or welcome this approach. In addition, the conflict perspective sees diversity as being two-dimensional: the haves and the have nots. Conflict theorists argue that athletes currently have little power and instead should have a major say in the organization of sport. There is no evidence in these case studies that sport managers attempt to distance themselves from the privileges of their positions and allow athletes to have a significant say in discussions about the future of their sport club or organization.

Although market forces play a role in their decision making, there is little evidence of sport managers using a conflict perspective. Conflict theory however assumes that all social practices are driven by primarily by (historical) market forces and tends to ignore how people organize social practices along the lines of other social relations such as gender, race, ethnicity, age, sexual preference, etc. A shift from a functional to a conflict perspective therefore, might not facilitate management of diversity in sport organizations.

Critical perspective

In discussing the functionalist and conflict perspectives in the previous sections, I used primarily the actions of actors described in this book as examples. This is not possible in the following discussion of critical perspectives because these are rarely used by the actors (except for the members of Faja Lobi in a limited way). A critical perspective assumes that historic, social and material forces shape social practices, that conflict and consensus can exist simultaneously (fragmentation), that consensus is never permanent, and, that sport (and society) are continually changing as historical, economic and social forces change (Coakley, 1998; Verweel, chapter 1; Verweel & de Ruijter, chapter 2). Sport is therefore not seen as separate from society but as part of it. It has no (eternal) essence because it is a social practice defined by those who practice it and therefore changes over time and context. The meanings that are assigned to sport in the case study about sport and international cooperative development illustrate this well (Boessenkool & van Eekeren, chapter 7); the sense making varies between organizations and within organizations. In other words, actors engage in sense making in context (Anthonissen & Boessenkool, 1998). Although a critical perspective assumes that there is no one essence that defines sport, it acknowledges that there is a dominant discourse that attempts to define that essence as we see throughout this book. The hegemonic nature of that discourse must continually be reinforced and reproduced by sport managers and administrators because it is continually challenged, as the case study of Faja Lobi (chapter 6) and the discussion about gender and organizations (chapter 3) suggest.

Yet a critical perspective goes further than looking solely at meanings produced by the actor in context. According to critical sociologists and anthropologists, sport is a social practice in which current economic, historical and social forces come together. They look critically at the way processes of definition and obtaining hegemony are related to social forces in society as a whole. Actors in interaction with each other create only part of the discourse about sport. A discourse is also constructed, reinforced and/or contested by the media, by the use of power, by the forces of economics, etc. (see Knoppers & Elling, 1999a for a discussion on the media). Most of the practices detailed in the case studies contribute to white male hegemony in sport. Yet that hegemony is 'leaky' as is illustrated by the struggle of women to be able to participate in sport or the efforts of 'immigrants' (and gays and lesbians) to set up their own clubs.

The following example about the organization of the modern Olympic Games illustrates how discourse and practice are interrelated. The modern Olympic Games were organized in 1896 based in part on dominant discourses about gender and social class (Cahn, 1994; Hargreaves, 1994). Competitive sport at that time was organized by and for men whose hobby was to participate in sport (amateurism). Participation in competitive sport was assumed to make 'men' out of (middle class) boys who grew up in a world that seemed to be becoming increasingly feminized. The rules for participation in competition reflected the interests of the higher social classes. The rules limited participation in organized competitive sport literally to gentlemen. Women and those who earned money through participation were not welcome. This led to a dual organizational form: men's amateur sport and professional sport.

Although 'amateurism' (*participating for the love of sport*) was the dominant discourse about sport at the turn of this century, those who wanted to earn their living through sport and those who wanted to use sport as a commercial tool countered with an alternate discourse about sport participation. This discourse linked sport participation to achievement and/or the best performance. Although de Coubertin, the founder of the modern Olympic Games, wanted the Games to be restricted to 'amateurs' (*it is not whether you win or lose but how you play the game*) the Olympic motto: *higher, faster, further* supported the alternate discourse. Capitalist forces of course, played an important role here too. Gradually competitive sport became defined as a practice about who is the fastest or the best, not about merely participating. The alternate discourse has been blended with the dominant discourse to form a discourse that says that the 'best' sport is about the 'best' performance. It is not surprising then that professional athletes became defined as the best athletes and that the word 'amateur' eventually became synonymous with 'just trying' or 'beginner.' This blended discourse gradually collapsed the boundaries between amateur and professional sport. Currently amateur and professional athletes compete together in the Olympic Games and for world titles. This is an example how discourse and practice are inseparably linked and inform each other to create, challenge or reproduce hegemony.

Critical sociologists and anthropologists assume that social life consists of struggles over the power to define (make sense) and to make that definition hegemonic. The chapter on professionalization is a good example of this struggle to define and to obtain hegemony. Sport managers have a particular vision about how a club should be organized and use various techniques such as persuasion and coercion (pressure from the media, the KNVB, and local government officials) to get their discourse accepted, in other words, for that discourse to become hegemonic (common sense) as the only way or best way of looking at and organizing sport. The alternate discourse of self defined achievement is marginalized.

To date, the critical sociological and anthropological perspective is rarely seen in sport practice. Possibly the number of alternate discourses has been few because the functional perspective is so dominant. As indicated earlier, the functional/integration perspective is so dominant that alternate discourses either get coopted or are marginalized in sport. Other ways of making sense of sport are often not heard. 'Organized sports were developed to emphasize competition, efficiency and performance ranking systems and to devalue supportiveness, kindness, responsiveness, and caring contributed to their 'gendered' character . . . Sports . . . have been socially constructed out of the values and experiences of [white heterosexual middle class] men. (Coakley, 1998, p. 45). The same can be said about sport organizations. Those who are marginalized in sport may have the room to experiment and to develop alternate discourses because they have little vested interest in the status quo. Perhaps it is in the margins where 'playing room' can be found to bring about change. This change, therefore, means moving to the margins and listening to the marginalized voices; their voices have been missing from the dominant discourses about sport. Without such a 'move', athletes who feel that their ways of making sense of sport are marginalized may move out of (formally) organized sport, organize their own sport experiences and/or drop out of sport altogether.

A step toward management of diversity

The goal of critical sociologists/anthropologists who look at sport is to make sport organizations not only more efficient and rational but more diverse and fair (see also Verweel & Anthonissen, chapter 6 in this book). The switch to using a critical lens is not easy. Most sport organizations and sport officials worldwide use a functionalist lens to look at sport. It is much easier to 'sell' sport as an instrument for integration or for national building than as a social practice that reinforces (and at times contests) inequitable social relations. A critical / cultural studies perspective requires us as managers and/or scholars to acknowledge the limits of our ways of seeing as they are influenced by our social positions as male or female, as black or white, as ethnic majority or minority, as gay or straight, etc. Obviously then this perspective is closely allied with the fragmentation perspective on culture in organizations (Martin, 1992).

We need therefore to think of managing diversity not only in terms of the assignment of meaning but also at the way the processes of obtaining hegemony and defining are related to social forces in society as a whole. What do the ways that the actors in this book assign meaning have to do with their social position? How is the incorporation of the diversity in the assignment of meaning limited by constraints due to social relations such as gender, social class, age and (dis)ability? What do the meanings sport managers assign to sport have to do with meanings they assign to the body and physical experiences and to their nonsport experiences? Moving towards management of diversity is therefore not solely a question of 'switching' conceptual perspectives but also a question of looking at power and ideology in a critical sense. The case studies suggest that sport managers see 'dysfunction' within their organization but frequently do not attend to differences because they are afraid to lose their position/power. Possibly managing diversity in the ways outlined in this book requires a different type of sport manager. It requires managers who understand that sameness and difference are not in opposition to each other but are dialectical, who encourage diversity among participants and managers, and who integrate the various meanings assigned to sport participation into the structure of the club.

Notes

1.   These 'places' or spaces are not necessarily equal as the case studies point out. Some meanings may receive a more central place in the story about the experience than others.

2.   KDP is a sport club with five sports. Each sport forms a separate section and has its own council. The chairs of the council represent their section in the council of the entire club.

3.   The football council consists of men, on the average 45 years old, who have been members of the club for a long time and have been members of the lower teams. The chair comes from a family that has a long tradition of chairing the football council.

4.   Interestingly, the Dutch Olympic Committee encourages clubs to increase their recreational and less competitive programs.

5.   Michels (1959) argues that organization implies oligarchy. 'In every organization, whether it be a political party, a professional union, or any other association of kind, the aristocratic tendency manifests itself very clearly. The mechanism of the organization, while conferring a solidarity structure, induces serious changes in the organized mass, completely inverting the respective position of the leaders and the led' (p. 32).

6.   Yet during election time, sport is framed as an important part of community building.

7.   The Dutch -English dictionary of Van Dale (1997) translates 'allochtoon' as 'immigrant, foreigner' and 'autochtoon' as 'indigenous, native.'   The Central Bureau for Statistics uses the terms 'allochtoon' and 'autochtoon' to denote those (or their parents) who are born outside and in the Netherlands respectively (CBS, 1996, p.23). Yet this distinction is problematic. First, people from the Dutch Antilles are Dutch citizens and therefore technically cannot be classified as 'allochtoon' or 'foreigner.' Surinam became independent only in 1975. Those born before that date and living in the Netherlands have always had Dutch citizenship. They are not 'foreigners.' Second, the Department of Health,

133

Well-being and Sport focuses its 'allochtoon' policies on people from Surinam, the Dutch Antilles, Turkey, Morocco and refugees (Elling & de Knop, 1999). People born in Germany, Norway or the United States for example, are not classified as 'allochtoon' and therefore not targeted in 'allochtoon' policies. Possibly skin colour plays a role with respect to who gets defined as 'allochtoon.'

Sometimes the term 'ethnic minority/majority' is used instead of the allochtoon/ autochtoon distinction. This term is preferred for example by the Department of Foreign Affairs (Redactie binnenland, 1999). 'Ethnic minority' can be defined in various ways: a low social position in Dutch society, limited chances of obtaining and/or developing political power over the course of several generations (SCP 1998, p. 235). Yet this term has not been used long enough to be clearly defined and adopted universally.

Making distinctions among social groups is therefore fraught with difficulties. In this chapter we have chosen to use the English translation of 'allochtoon' and 'autochtoon' using 'immigrant' and 'nonimmigrant' respectively. We have placed them in quotation marks to show that they are questionable terms. Who is a 'nonimmigrant' or who is an 'immigrant'?

8. In 1997 there were 1,435,000 'immigrant' born people living in the NL. The largest groups are from Surinam (287,000), Turkey (280,000), Morocco (233,000) and the Dutch Antilles/Aruba (95,000) (SCP, 1998, pp. 241).

9. This is also true for lesbians and gays (Elling & de Knop, 1999)

10. The deficiency model is often used is sport when gender differences are discussed. Women are seen as 'deficient' when compared with men (Knoppers, 1999).

11. This was evident in the interest shown in the symposium about sport and ICD. The Centre for Policy and Management of the University of Utrecht in cooperation with the Departments of Foreign Affairs and of Health, Welfare and Sport, organized a symposium 'Sport and international development', on January 16, 1998. More than 100 representatives from sport, ICD, the government and higher education attended. The conclusions of this symposium were incorporated in the policy paper 'Sport in development: Team work scores! ' Those who attended showed interest in the role sport plays in African society.

The government, represented by former government leaders Terpstra and Pronk, used this interest to develop the first policy statement about this subject: 'Sport and development: Team work scores!' (Pronk & Terpstra, 1998).

References

Acker, J. (1990) Hierarchies, jobs, bodies: A theory of gendered organizations. *Gender & Society, 4,* 139-158.

Acker, J. (1992) Gendering organizational theory. In A. J. Mills and P. Tancred (Eds.), *Gendering organizational analysis.* Newbury Park, CA: Sage, pp. 248 - 262.

Acker, J. (1995) Feminist goals and organizing processes. In M.M. Ferree & P.Y. Martin (Eds.) *Feminist organizations: Harvest of the new women's movement.* Philadelphia: Temple University Press, pp. 137 - 144.

Acosta, R. & Carpenter, L. (1998) *Women in intercollegiate sport: A longitudinal study - twenty one year update, 1977 - 1998. Report.* Brooklyn, NY 11210: Department of Physical Education and Exercise Science.

Andrews, D. (1998) Feminizing Olympic reality. *International Review for Sociology of Sport,* 33: 5- 18.

Anthonissen, A. (1997) *Tussen bierviltje en floppydisk* (Between beer coaster and floppy disk). Arnhem: NOC*NSF.

Anthonissen, A. and Boessenkool, J. (1996) *De sportvereniging tussen traditie en commercie* (The sport club between tradition and commerce) Arnhem: NOC*NSF.

Anthonissen, A. and Boessenkool, J. (1998) *Betekenissen van Besturen: variaties in bestuurlijk handelen in amateursportorganisaties,* (Meanings in management: Variations in the managing of amateur sport organizations). Utrecht: ISOR.

Appadurai, A. (1990) Disjuncture and difference in the global cultural economy. In M. Featherstone (Ed), *Global culture: Nationalism, globalization and modernity.* London: Sage, pp. 295-310.

Baal, J. van (1974) *De agressie der gelijken,* (The aggression of equals) Assen: Van Gorcum.

Bailey, F.G. (1977) *Morality and expediency: The folklore of academic politics.* Oxford: Basil Blackwell.

Bauman, Z. (1990) 'Modernity and ambivalence. In M. Featherstone (ed.) *Globalculture: Nationalism, globalization and modernity.* London: Sage, pp. 143-170.

Benschop, Y. (1996) *De mantel der gelijkheid: Gender in organisaties.*(The coat of equality: Gender in organizations). Assen: Van Gorcum.

Blommaert, J. (1995) Ideologies in intercultural communication. In O. Dahl, (Ed.) *Intercultural communication and contact.*. Stavanger: Misjonshogskolens Forlag, pp.9-27.

Boyle, M. and McKay, J. (1995) 'You leave your troubles at the gate': A case study of the exploitation of older women's labor and 'leisure' in sport. *Gender & Society, 9*, 556 - 575.

Brenner, Y.S. (1996) *Looking back.*. Utrecht: University of Utrecht.

Brink, G. van den (1978) Ideologie en hegemonie bij Gramsci (Ideology and hegemony according to Gramsci). In H. Boekraad and H. Hoeks (Eds.) *Te elfer ure* (The eleventh hour). Nijmegen: Socialistische uitgeverij, pp.10-58.

Burgers, J. , Reinsch, P., Snel, E. and Tak, H. (1998) *Burgers als ieder ander: Een advies inzake lokaal beleid en minderheden.* (Citizens like everyone else: A recommendation for local policy and ethnic minorities). Utrecht: Universiteit Utrecht.

Cahn, S. (1994) *Coming on strong: Gender and sexuality in twentieth-century women's sport.* New York: Free Press, Macmillan.

Calás, M. B. and Smircich, L. (1992a) Re-writing gender into organizational theorizing: Directions from feminist perspectives. In M. Reed and M. Hughes (Eds.), *Rethinking organization: New directions in organization theory and analysis.* London: Sage, pp. 227-253.

Calás, M. B. and Smircich, L. (1992b). Using the 'F' word: Feminist theories and the social consequences of organizational research. In A. J. Mills and P. Tancred (Eds.), *Gendering organizational analysis.* Newbury Park, CA: Sage, pp. 222-234.

CBS (1996) Statistisch Jaarboek 1996 (Statistical yearbook 1996). Voorburg: Centraal Burau Statistiek

Coakley, J. (1998) *Sport in society: Issues and controversies.* (6th ed.) London: McGraw-Hill.

Cockburn, C. (1991) *In the way of women: Men's resistance to sex equality in organizations.* Ithaca: ILR Press.

Collinson, D. and Collinson, M (1992) Mismanaging sexual harassment: Protecting the perpetrator and blaming the victim. *Women in Management Review, 7*, 11 -17.

Collinson, D. & Hearn, J. (1994) Naming men as men: Implications for work, organization and management, *Gender, Work and Organization, 1*, 2 -22.

Connell, R.W. (1987). *Gender & power.* Stanford, California: Stanford University Press.

138

Connell, R. W. (1995). *Masculinities*. Berkeley: University of California Press.

Deal, T. and Kennedy, A. (1982) *Corporate cultures. The rites and rituals of corporate life*. MA, USA: Addison-Wesley.

Digel, H. and P.Fornoff (1989) *Sport in der Entwicklungszusammenarbeit*. (Sport in international development) München: Weltforum-Verlag.

Dossier (1999, March): *Work, time, pay and gender. 1999 Employment guidelines*. Quarterly magazine of the Community action Programme on equal opportunities for women and men, no. 7.

Douglas, M. (1982) *Essays with sociology of perception*. London: Routledge

Du Gay, P. (1977) *Production of Culture, cultures of production*. London: Sage

Durkheim, E. (1893) De la division du travail social.

Duyvendak, J.W. (1998) *Integratie door sport*. (Integration through sport.) Rotterdam: Bestuursdienst Rotterdam.

Eekeren, F. van (1997) *Coach the coaches. Onderzoek naar een sportontwikkelingsproject in Zuid-Afrika*. (Coach the coaches: Research on a sport project in South Africa). Utrecht: Center for Policy and Management, University of Utrecht

Elling, A. and de Knop, P. (1999) *Naar eigen wensen en mogelijkheden*. (According to one's own wishes and possibilities). Arnhem: NOC*NSF.

Emancipatieraad (1997) *Sport & gender: Vrouwen in beeld*. (Sport & gender: Women in the picture). Den Haag: Ministrie van Sociale Zaken, Advies en Onderzoek.

Entzinger, H. (1998) Het voorportaal van Nederland. (The gateway to the Netherlands). In K. Geuijen (Ed.) *Multi-culturalisme*. Utrecht: Lemma, pp. 67 -80.

Equality (1999) Nederland kan voorbeeld nemen aan Europa. (The Netherlands can use Europe as an example.) *Equality matters, 1* (2), p. 2.

Expert meeting (minutes) (1998) Gender, ethnicity and the sport media. December 11, Hilversum: NOS.

Foster, J. (1999) An invitation to dialogue: Clarifying the position of feminist gender theory in relation to sexual difference theory. *Gender & Society, 13*, 431 - 456.

Friedman, C. (1995) *Cultural identity and global processes*. London: Sage.

Giddens, A. (1979) *Central problems in social theory*. London, Mac Millan Press.

Giddens, A. (1984) *The constitution of society*. Cambridge: Polity Press.

Giddens, A. (1990) *The consequences of modernity*. London: Polity Press.

Goffman, E. (1961) *Asylums: Essays on the social situation of mental patients and other inmates*. New York: Doubleday/Anchor Press.

Gunsteren, H.R. van (1992) *Eigentijds Burgerschap.* (Modern citizenship). The Hague: SDU, Wrr publication.

Hall, M.A. (1996). *Feminism and sporting bodies: Essays on theory and practice.* Champaign, IL: Human Kinetics.

Hall, M. A., Cullen, D. and Slack, T. (1990) *The gender structure of national sport organizations.* Sport Canada: Occasional Papers, volume 2 (1) Ottawa, Canada: Government of Canada, Fitness and Amateur Sport.

Hargreaves, Jennifer. (1994) *Sporting females: Critical issues in the history and sociology of women's sports.* London: Routledge.

Hargreaves, John and Tomlinson, A. (1992) Getting there: Cultural theory and the sociological analysis of sport in Britain, *Sociology of Sport Journal, 9,* 207-219.

Hearn, J. and Parkin, W. (1983) Gender and organizations: A selective review and a critique of a neglected area. *Organization Studies, 4,* 219- 242.

Hearn, J. and Parkin, W. (1987) *'Sex' at work: The power and paradox of organization sexuality.* New York: St. Martin's Press.

Hoek, S. van and Veen, F. van (1997) Elke oogopslag, elke huidskleur, elke beweging kan kwetsend zijn. (Each eye movement, each skin color, each movement can hurt someone.) *De Volkskrant, 76,* 18 October , p. 9.

Hofstede, G. (1992) *Allemaal andersdenkenden.* (Everyone thinks differently). Amsterdam: Contact.

Horch, H.D. (1994), Resource composition and oligarchization, *European Journal for Sport Management, 1/2 ,* pages not available.

Human, L. (1998) *De winst van diversiteit: Naar een effectieve visie op intercultureel management.* (The positive effect of diversity: Towards an effective vision on intercultural management.) Utrecht: Forum.

Ibsen, B. (1997) *Change in voluntary sector in sport..* Paper presented at the ISSA symposium Oslo ; The Danish State Institute of Physical Education

Janssens, J. (1998) *Etnische tweedeling in de sport.* (Ethnic separation in sport). Arnhem: NOC*NSF.

Kalb, D. (1997) The limits of the new social orthodoxy. *Focaal: Tijdschrijft voor de Antropologie nr.30-31. ,* 236 - 260.

Kanter, R.M. (1977) *Men and women of the corporation.* New York: Basic Books.

Kanter, R.M. (1984) *The change masters: Corporate entrepreneurs at work.* London: Allen Unwin.

Kearny, A. T. (1992) *Sport als inspiratiebron voor de samenleving,* (Sport as inspiration for society). Arnhem: NOC*NSF.

Knoppers, A. (1987). Gender and the coaching profession. *Quest, 39,* 9-22.

Knoppers, A. (1992) Explaining male dominance and sex segregation in coaching: Three perspectives. *Quest, 44*, 210-227.

Knoppers, A. (1999) 'Voorhoede van Ajax speelt meisjesvoetbal': Gender en voetbal. (Offense of Ajax plays girls' football: Gender and football). *Tijdschrift voor Gender Studies., 2 (4)*.

Knoppers, A. and Bouman, Y. (1996). *Trainers/coaches: Een kwestie van kwaliteit* (Trainers/coaches: A question of quality?). Papendal, Arnhem: NOC*NSF.

Knoppers, A. & Bouman, Y. (1998). *Altijd beter dan mijn sporters* (Always better than my athletes). Papendal, Arnhem: NOC*NSF.

Knoppers, A. and Elling, A. (1999a) *Gender, etniciteit en de sportmedia.* (Gender, ethnicity and the sport media.) Utrecht/Tilburg: Center for Policy and Management, University of Utrecht; Leisure Studies, University of Tilburg, the Netherlands.

Knoppers, A. and Elling, A. (1999b). *Het is leuker om zelf te voetballen: Beeldvorming over de trainersfunctie in voetbal.* (It is more fun to play: images about football coaches) Zeist: KNVB.

Koot, W. and Hogema, I. (1992) *Organisatiecultuur: Fictie en werkelijkheid* (Organizational culture: Fiction and reality). Muiderberg: Coutinho.

Lagendijk, E. and Gugten, M. van der (1996) *Sport en allochtonen.* (Sport and immigrants) Rijswijk: Ministerie van VWS.

Latour, B. (1994) *Wij zijn nooit modern geweest. Pleidooi voor een symmetrische antropologie* (We were never modern: Plea for a symetrical anthropology) Rotterdam: Van Gennep.

Leidner, R. (1991) Serving hamburgers and selling insurance: Gender, work and identity in interactive service jobs. *Gender & Society, 5*, 154 - 177.

Lorber, J. (1993). Believing is seeing: Biology as ideology. *Gender & Society, 7*, 568-581.

Macintosh, D. and Whitson, D. (1990) *The game planners: Transforming Canada's sport system.* Montreal: McGill - Queen's University Press.

Malkki, L. (1992), National geographic: The rooting of peoples and the territorialization of national identity among scholars and refugees, *Cultural Antropology 7* (1), 24-44.

Martin, J. (1992) *Cultures in organizations. Three perspectives.* New York: Oxford University Press .

McKay, J. (1993) Masculine hegemony, the state and the politics of gender equity policy research. *Culture and Policy, 5*, 223 - 240.

McLuhan, M. (1964) *Understanding media..* New York: McGraw-Hill.

Messner, M. (1988). Sport and male domination: The female athlete as contested ideological terrain. *Sociology of Sport Journal, 5*, 197-211.

Messner, M. (1992). *Power at play: Sports and the problem of masculinity.* Boston: Beacon Press.

Nederveen Pieterse, J. (1996) Globalisation and culture: Three paradigms. *Economic and Political Weekly, nr.* 23, 1389-1393.

Niphuis-Nell, M. (Ed.) (1997) *Sociale atlas van de vrouw. Deel 4.* (Social atlas of women; part 4) Rijswijk: Sociaal Cultureel Planbureau.

NOC*NSF (1998), Meerjarenbeleidsplan 1998-2002 (Policy plan 1998 -2002) *Tijd voor Vrijwilligersbeleid,* Arnhem: NOC*NSF.

Ouchi, W. (1978) Markets, bureaucracies and clans. *Administrative Science Quarterly,* vol.25, pp. 129-141.

Peters T. and Waterman, R. (1982) *In search of excellence.* New York: Harper and Row.

Pringle, R. (1989) *Secretaries talk: Sexuality, power and work..* New York: Versco.

Pronk, J. and Terpstra, E. (1998) *Sport in ontwikkeling: Samenspel scoort!* (Sport in development: Team work scores!) Den Haag: Ministerie van Buitenlandse Zaken en Ministerie van VWS .

Ramsay, K. and Parker, M. (1992) Gender, bureaucracy and organizational culture. In M. Savage and A. Witz (Eds.), *Gender and bureaucracy.* Oxford: Blackwell Publishers, pp. 253 - 276.

Redactie Binnenland (1999) Woorden: Allochtoon. (Words: Foreigner) *Trouw, 57 (16901*), 4.

Reskin, B. (1988) Bringing the men back in: Sex differentiation and the devaluation of women's work. *Gender & Society, 2*, 58-81.

Robertson, R. (1992) *Globalization: Social theory and global culture.* London: Sage.

Robertson, R. (1995),Glocalization: Time-space and homogeneity-heterogeneity. In M. Featherstone, S. Lash & R. Robertson (Eds.) *Global modernities.* London: Sage London, pp. 25-44.

Roosevelt, T.R. (1993) Managing diversity. In Anne Frank Stichting (Ed.) *De multiculturel organisatie en het belang van intercultureel management.* (The multicultural organization and the importance of intercultural management). Deventer: Kluwer.

Rubingh, B. and Westerbeek, H.M. (1992) Besturen van een sportvereniging (Managing a sport club). *Spel en sport, 1,* 2-7.

Ruijter, A. de (1995) Cultural pluralism and citizenship. *Culture Dynamics, 7(2),* 215 -232.

Salet, W. (1996) *De conditie van stedelijkheid en het vraagstuk van maatschappelijke integratie* (The urban condition and the issue of societal integration). Den Haag: VUGA.

SCP (1998) *Sociaal en Cultureel Rapport*. Rijswijk: Sociaal Cultureel Planbureau.

Slack, T. (1997) *Understanding sport organizations*. Champaign, IL. : Human Kinetics.

Slack, T. and Hinings, B. (1992) Understanding change in national sport organizations: An integration of theoretical perspectives. *Journal of Sport Management, 6,* pp. 114-132.

Smirchich, L. (1983) Concepts of Culture and organizational analysis. *Administrative Science Quarterly*, vol.28, pp. 339-358.

Spiro, M.E. (1966) Buddhism and economic action in Birma. *American Anthropologist 68*, pp. 1163-1173.

Spradley, J.P. (1972) Foundations of cultural knowledge. In J.P. Spradley (Ed.) *Culture and cognition: Rules maps and plans*. San Fransisco, CA: Chandler, pp. 3-41.

Stol, P. (1995) *Opsporing verzocht: Vrouwelijke trainers/coaches! (A search is needed: Women coaches!)* Stage-onderzoek in opdracht van NOC*NSF. Universiteit Utrecht, Tracé Sport, Bewegen en Gezondheid, vakgroep Pedagogiek.

Swank, M. (1996) *Voetbalvereniging Faja Lobi*. (Football club Faja Lobi). Utrecht: Centrum voor Beleid en Management, Universiteit Utrecht.

Swank, M. And van Eekeren, F. (1998) *Sport en ontwikkelingssamenwerking. Verslag van het symposium*. (Sport and international development: A symposium report.) Utrecht: CBM en DVL/OS .

Tolson, A. (1996) *Mediations: Text and discourse in media studies*. Arnold Publishing Co.

Trice, H.M. and Beyer, J.M. (1993) *The Culture of work organizations*. Englewood Cliffs/New Jersey: Prentice Hall .

Verweel, P. (1987) *Universiteit: Verandering en planning* (University: Changing and planning). ICAU mededelingen no 28, Utrecht: SWP.

Verweel, P. (1995) *Beeld en zelfbeeld van een allochtone vereniging*. (Image and self image of an immigrant club). Utrecht: Centrum voor Beleid en Management, Universiteit Utrecht.

Verweel, P. (1998) De multiculturele organisatie. (The multicultural organization.) In K. Geuijen (Ed.) *Multiculturalisme*. Utrecht: Lemma, pp. 129 - 146.

Verweel, P. and David, K. (1995) *Verborgen dimensies: cultuur en macht in fusies* (Hidden dimensions: Culture and power in mergers). Utrecht: SWP.

Vink N. and Schapink, D. (1994) Lerende organisaties in ontwikkelingssamenwerking. (Learning organizations in international development). In W. Koot, W. and J. Boessenkool (Eds.) *Management & Organisatie* Themanummer Intercultureel Management. Alphen aan de Rijn: Samson.

Wallace, A.F.C. (1962) *Culture and Personality*. New York: Random House.

Wallerstein, I. (1975) *The modern world system*. New York: Academic Press, p.13-26.

Weick, K. (1995) *Sense making in organizations*. London: Sage Publications.

Witz, A. and Savage, M. (1992). The gender of organizations. In M. Savage and A. Witz (Eds.), *Gender and bureaucracy*. Oxford: Blackwell Publishers, pp. 3 -60.

About the authors

Dr. Anton Anthonissen is a social-cultural scholar who has done extensive research on sport organizations at the local and national level. His current research focuses on multi-culturalism in sport organizations and management.

Dr. Jan Boessenkool is an organizational anthropologist and an experienced researcher in the area of sport. He has been involved in various projects in African countries for ten years. His research focuses on the management and organization of sport clubs.

Drs. Frank van Eekeren is a researcher and lecturer who looks at sport organizations through the lens of intercultural management and international cooperative development. Currently he is exploring processes of multi-culturalism in sport organizations. He is a member of the board of the Foundation for African Sports Development (FASD) and works as a volunteer at a football club.

Dr. Annelies Knoppers is a sociologist and a researcher in the area of gender and (sport) organizations. She has conducted research in the USA and the Netherlands that explores the position of coaches, the culture coaches create, the images soccer players and coaches have of 'coaches', and, the meanings given to gender and ethnicity by the sport media.

Prof. dr. Arie de Ruijter is professor of cultural and social anthropology at the University of Utrecht and director of the national research school CERES. He has published extensively in the areas of theory and general methodology in the social sciences and on multiculturalism and identity.

Prof. dr. Paul Verweel is professor of organization and policy from a multicultural perspective, and Chair of the Center of Policy and Management, University Utrecht (CBM). His areas of expertise include diversity in organizations, mergers, strategic management, organizational culture and dynamics, and the construction of meaning. He is a member of various national and local advisory boards of sport organizations.